WHAT ALL
THE WORLD'S A-SEEKING

WHAT ALL
THE WORLD'S A-SEEKING

OR

The Vital Law of True Life,
True Greatness, Power and Happiness

RALIPH WALDO TRINE

MANOR
ROCKVILLE, MARYLAND
2008

ISBN: 978-1-60450-118-6

Published by Arc Manor
P. O. Box 10339
Rockville, MD 20849-0339
www.ArcManor.com
Printed in the United States of America/United Kingdom

CONTENTS

PREFACE

THERE are two reasons the author has for putting forth this little volume: he feels that the time is, as it always has been, ripe for it; and second, his soul has ever longed to express itself upon this endless theme. It therefore comes from the heart – the basis of his belief that it will reach the heart.

R.W.T.
Boston,
Massachusetts

PREFACE TO REVISED EDITION

IT is impossible for one in a single volume, or perhaps in a number of volumes, to reach the exact needs of every reader.

It is always a source of gratitude, as well as of inspiration for better and more earnest work in the future, for one to know that the truths that have been and that are so valuable and so vital to him he has succeeded in presenting in a manner such that they prove likewise of value to others. The author is most grateful for the good, kind words that have come so generously from so many hundreds of readers of this simple little volume from all parts of the world. He is also grateful to that large company of people who have been so good as to put the book into the hands of so many others.

And as the days have passed, he has not been unmindful of the fact that he might make it, when the time came, of still greater value to many. In addition to a general revision of the book, some four or five questions that seemed to be most frequently asked he has endeavored to point answer to in an added part of some thirty pages, under the general title, "Character-building Thought Power." The volume enters therefore upon its fifteenth thousand better able, possibly, to come a little more directly in touch with the every-day needs of those who will be sufficiently interested to read it.

R.W.T.
Sunnybrae Farm
Croton-on-the-Hudson
New York

Part I

The Principle

Would you find that wonderful life supernal,
That life so abounding, so rich, and so free?
Seek then the laws of the Spirit Eternal,
With them bring your life into harmony.

*H*ow can I make life yield its fullest and best? How can I know the true secret of power? How can I attain to a true and lasting greatness? How can I fill the whole of life with a happiness, a peace, a joy, a satisfaction that is ever rich and abiding, that ever increases, never diminishes, that imparts to it a sparkle that never loses its lustre, that ever fascinates, never wearies?

No questions, perhaps, in this form or in that have been asked oftener than these. Millions in the past have asked them. Millions are asking them to-day. They will be asked by millions yet unborn. Is there an answer, a true and safe one for the millions who are eagerly and longingly seeking for it in all parts of the world to-day, and for the millions yet unborn who will as eagerly strive to find it as the years come and go? Are you interested, my dear reader, in the answer? The fact that you have read even thus far in this little volume whose title has led you to take it up, indicates that you are, – that you are but one of the innumerable company already mentioned.

It is but another way of asking that great question that has come through all the ages – What is the *summum bonum* in life? and there have been countless numbers who gladly would have given all they possessed to have had the true and satisfactory answer. Can we then find this answer, true and satisfactory to ourselves, surely the brief time spent together must be counted as the most precious and valuable of life itself. *There is an answer:* follow closely, and that our findings may be the more conclusive, take issue with me at every step if you choose, but tell me finally if it is not true and satisfactory.

There is one great, one simple principle, which, if firmly laid hold of, and if made the great central principle in one's life, around which all others properly arrange and subordinate themselves, will make that life a grand success, truly great and genuinely happy, loved and blessed by all in just the degree in which it is laid hold upon, – a principle which, if universally made thus, would wonderfully change this old world in which we live, – ay, that would transform it almost in a night, and it is for its coming that the world has long been waiting; that in place of the gloom and despair in almost countless numbers of lives would bring light and hope and contentment, and no longer would it be said as so truly to-day, that "man's inhumanity to man, makes countless thousands mourn"; that would bring to the life of the fashionable society woman, now spending her days and her nights in seeking for nothing but her own pleasure, such a flood of true and genuine pleasure and happiness and satisfaction as would make the poor, weak something she calls by this name so pale before it, that she would quickly see that she hasn't known what true pleasure is, and that what she has been mistaking for the real, the genuine, is but as a baser metal compared to the purest of gold, as a bit of cut glass compared to the rarest of diamonds, and that would make this same woman who scarcely deigns to notice the poor woman who washes her front steps, but who, were the facts known, may be living a much grander life, and consequently of much more value to the world than she herself, see that this poor woman is after all her sister, because child of the same Father; and that would make the humble life of this same poor woman beautiful and happy and sweet in its humility; that would give us a nation of statesmen in place of, with now and then an exception, a nation of politicians, each one bent upon his own personal aggrandizement at the expense of the general good; that would go far, ay, very far toward solving our great and hard-pressing social problems with which we are already face to face; that, in short, would make each man a prince among men, and each woman a queen among women.

I have seen the supreme happiness in lives where this principle has been caught and laid hold of, some, lives that seemed not to have much in them before, but which under its wonderful influences have been so transformed and so beautified, that have been made so sweet and so strong, so useful and so precious, that each day seems to them all too short, the same time that before, when they could scarcely see what was in life to make it worth the living, dragged wearily along. So there are countless numbers of people in the world with lives that seem not to have much in them, among the wealthy classes and among the poorer, who might under the influence of this great, this simple principle, make them so precious, so rich, and so happy that time would seem only too short, and they would wonder why they have been so long running on the wrong track, for it is true that much the larger portion of the world to-day is on the wrong track in the pursuit of happiness; but almost all are there, let it be said, not through choice, but by reason of not knowing the right, the true one.

The fact that really great, true, and happy lives have been lived in the past and are being lived to-day gives us our starting-point. Time and again I have examined such lives in a most careful endeavor to find what has made them so, and have found that in *each and every* individual case this that we have now come to has been the great central principle upon which they have been built. I have also found that in numbers of lives where it has not been, but where almost every effort apart from it has been made to make them great, true, and happy, they have not been so; and also that no life built upon it in sufficient degree, other things being equal, has failed in being thus.

Let us then to the answer, examine it closely, see if it will stand every test, if it is the true one, and if so, rejoice that we have found it, lay hold of it, build upon it, tell others of it. The last four words have already entered us at the open door. The idea has prevailed in the past, and this idea has dominated the world, that *self* is the great concern, – that if one would find success, greatness, happiness, he must give all attention to self, and to self alone. This has been the great mistake, this the fatal error, this the *direct* opposite of the right, the true as set forth in the great immutable law that – *we find our own lives in losing them in the service of others,* in longer form – the more of our lives we give to others, the fuller and the richer, the greater and the grander, the more beautiful and the more happy our own lives become. It is as that great and sweet soul who when with us lived at Concord said, – that generous giving or losing of your life which saves it.

This is an expression of one of the greatest truths, of one of the greatest principles of practical ethics the world has thus far seen. In a single word, it is *service*, – not self but the other self. We shall soon see, however, that our love, our service, our helpfulness to others, invariably comes back to us, intensified sometimes a hundred or a thousand or a thousand thousand fold, and this by a great, immutable law.

The Master Teacher, he who so many years ago in that far-away Eastern land, now in the hill country, now in the lake country, as the people gathered round him, taught them those great, high-born, and tender truths of human life and destiny, the Christ Jesus, said identically this when he said and so continually repeated, – "He that is greatest among you shall be your servant"; and his whole life was but an embodiment of this principle or truth, with the result that the greatest name in the world to-day is his, – the name of him who as his life-work, healed the sick; clothed the naked; bound up the broken-hearted; sustained the weak, the faltering; befriended and aided the poor, the needy; condemned the proud, the vain, the selfish; and through it all taught the people to love justice and mercy and service, to live in their higher, their diviner selves, – in brief, to *live* his life, the Christ-life, and who has helped in making it possible for this greatest principle of practical ethics the world has thus far seen to be enunciated, to be laid hold of, to be lived by to-day. "He that is greatest among you shall be your servant," or, he who would be truly great and recognized as such must find it in the capacity of a servant.

And what, let us ask, is a servant? One who renders service. To himself? Never. To others? Alway. Freed of its associations and looked at in the light of its right and true meaning, than the word "servant" there is no greater in the language; and in this right use of the term, as we shall soon see, every life that has been really true, great, and happy has been that of a servant, and apart from this no such life *ever has been or ever can be lived.*

O you who are seeking for power, for place, for happiness, for contentment in the ordinary way, tarry for a moment, see that you are on the wrong track, grasp this great eternal truth, lay hold of it, and you will see that your advance along this very line will be manifold times more rapid. Are you seeking, then, to make for yourself a name? Unless you grasp this mighty truth and make your life accordingly, as the great clock of time ticks on and all things come to their proper level according to their merits, as all invariably, inevitably do, you will indeed be somewhat surprised to find how low, how very low your level is. Your name and your memory will be forgotten long ere the minute-hand has passed even a single time across the great dial; while your fellow-man who has grasped this simple but this great and all-necessary truth, and who accordingly is forgetting himself in the service of others, who is making his life a part of a hundred or a thousand or a million lives, thus illimitably intensifying or multiplying his own, instead of living as you in what otherwise would be his own little, diminutive self, will find himself ascending higher and higher until he stands as one among the few, and will find a peace, a happiness, a satisfaction so rich and so beautiful, com-pared to which yours will be but a poor miserable something, and whose name and memory when his life here is finished, will live in the minds and hearts of his fellow-men and of mankind fixed and eternal as the stars.

A corollary of the great principle already enunciated might be formulated thus: *there is no such thing as finding true happiness by searching for it directly*. It must come, if it come at all, indirect-ly, or by the service, the love, and the happiness we give to others. So, *there is no such thing as finding true greatness by searching for it directly*. It always, without a single exception has come indi-rectly in this same way, and it is not at all probable that this great eternal law is going to be changed to suit any particular case or cases. Then recognize it, put your life into harmony with it, and reap the rewards of its observance, or fail to recognize it and pay the penalty accordingly; for the law itself will remain unchanged.

The men and women whose names we honor and celebrate are invariably those with lives founded primarily upon this great law. Note if you will, every *truly* great life in the world's history, among those living and among the so-called dead, and tell me if in *every* case that life is not a life spent in the service of others, either direct-ly, or indirectly as when we say – he served his country. Whenever one seeks for reputation, for fame, for honor, for happiness directly and for his own sake, then that which is true and genuine never comes, at least to any degree worthy the name. It may seem to for a time, but a great law says that such an one gets so far and no farther. Sooner or later, generally sooner, there comes an end.

Human nature seems to run in this way, seems to be governed by a great paradoxical law which says, that whenever a man self-centred, thinking of, living for and in himself, is very desirous for place, for preferment, for honor, the very fact of his being thus is of itself a sufficient indicator that he is too small to have them, and mankind refuses to accord them. While the one who forgets self, and who, losing sight of these things, makes it his chief aim in life to help, to aid, and to serve others, by this very fact makes it known that he is large enough, is great enough to have them, and his fellow-men instinctively bestow them upon him. This is a great law which many would profit by to recognize. That it is true is attested by the fact that the praise of mankind instinctively and universally goes out to a hero; but who ever heard of a hero who became such by doing something for himself? Always something he has done for others. By the fact that monuments and statues are gratefully erected to the memory of those who have helped and served their fellow-men, not to those who have lived to themselves alone.

I have seen many monuments and statues erected to the memories of philanthropists, but I never yet have seen one erected to a miser; many to generous-hearted, noble-hearted men, but never yet to one whose whole life was that of a sharp bargain-driver, and who clung with a sort of semi-idiotic grasp to all that came thus into his temporary possession. I have seen many erected to statesmen, – statesmen, – but never one to mere politicians; many to true orators, but never to mere demagogues; many to soldiers and leaders, but never to men who were not willing, when necessary, to risk all in the service of their country. No, you will find that the world's monuments and statues have been erected and its praises and honors have gone out to those who were large and great enough to forget themselves in the service of others, who have been servants, true servants of mankind, who have been true to the great law that we find our own lives in losing them in the service of others. Not honor for themselves, but service for others. But notice the strange, wonderful, beautiful transformation as it returns upon itself, – *honor for themselves, because of service to others.*

It would be a matter of exceeding great interest to verify the truth of what has just been said by looking at a number of those who are regarded as the world's great sons and daughters, – those to whom its honors, its praises, its homage go out, – to see why it is, upon what their lives have been founded that they have become so great and are so honored. Of all this glorious company that would come up, we must be contented to look at but one or two.

There comes to my mind the name and figure of him the celebration of whose birthday I predict will soon be made a national holiday, – he than whom there is no greater, whose praises are sung and whose name and memory are honored and blessed by millions in all parts of the world to-day, and will be by millions yet unborn, our beloved and sainted Lincoln. And then I ask, Why is this? Why is this? One sentence of his tells us what to look to for the answer. During that famous series of public debates in Illinois with Stephen A. Douglas in 1858, speaking at Freeport, Mr. Douglas at one place said, "I care not whether slavery in the Territories be voted up or whether it be voted down, it makes not a particle of difference with me." Mr. Lincoln, speaking from the fulness of his great and royal heart, in reply said, with emotion, "I am sorry to perceive that my friend Judge Douglas is so constituted that he does not feel the lash the least bit when it is laid upon another man's back." Thoughts upon self? Not for a moment. Upon others? Always. He at once recognized in those black men four million brothers for whom he had a service to perform.

It would seem almost grotesque to use the word *self-ish* in connection with this great name. He very early, and when still in a very humble and lowly station in life, either consciously or unconsciously grasped this great truth, and in making the great underlying principle of his life to serve, to help his fellow-men, he adopted just that course that has made him one of the greatest of the sons of men, our royal-hearted elder brother. He never spent time in asking what he could do to attain to greatness, to popularity, to power, what to perpetuate his name and memory. He simply asked how he could help, how he could be of service to his fellow-men, and continually did all his hands found to do.

He simply put his life into harmony with this great principle; and in so doing he adopted the best means, – the *only* means to secure that which countless numbers seek and strive for directly, and every time so woefully fail in finding.

There comes to my mind in this same connection another princely soul, one who loved all the world, one whom all the world loves and delights to honor. There comes to mind also a little incident that will furnish an insight into the reason of it all. On an afternoon not long ago, Mrs. Henry Ward Beecher was telling me of some of the characteristics of Brooklyn's great preacher. While she was yet speaking of some of those along the very lines we are considering, an old gentleman, a neighbor, came into the room bearing in his hands something he had brought from Mr. Beecher's grave. It was the day next following Decoration Day. His story was this: As the great procession was moving into the cemetery with its bands of rich music, with its carriages laden with sweet and fragrant flowers, with its waving flags, beautiful in the sunlight, a poor and humble-looking woman with two companions, by her apparent nervousness attracted the attention of the gate-keeper. He kept her in view for a little while, and presently saw her as she gave something she had partially concealed to one of her companions, who, leaving the procession, went over to the grave of Mr. Beecher, and tenderly laid it there. Reverently she stood for a moment or two, and then, retracing her steps, joined her two companions, who with bowed heads were waiting by the wayside.

It was this that the old gentleman had brought, – a gold frame, and in it a poem cut from a volume, a singularly beautiful poem through which was breathed the spirit of love and service and self-devotion to the good and the needs of others. At one or two places where it fitted, the pen had been drawn across a word and Mr. Beecher's name inserted, which served to give it a still more real, vivid, and tender meaning. At the bottom this only was written, "From a poor Hebrew woman to the immortal friend of the Hebrews." There was no name, but this was sufficient to tell the whole story. Some poor, humble woman, but one out of a mighty number whom he had at some time befriended or helped or cheered, whose burden he had helped to carry, and soon perhaps had forgotten all about it. When we remember that this was his life, is it at all necessary to seek farther why all the world delights to honor this, another royal-hearted elder brother? and, as we think of this simple, beautiful, and touching incident, how true and living becomes the thought in the old, old lines! –

"Cast thy bread upon the waters, waft it on with praying breath,
In some distant, doubtful moment it may save a soul from death.
When you sleep in solemn silence, 'neath the morn and evening dew,
Stranger hands which you have strengthened may strew lilies over you."

Our good friend, Henry Drummond, in one of his most beautiful and valuable little works says – and how admirably and how truly! – that "love is the greatest thing in the world." Have you this greatest thing? Yes. How, then, does it manifest itself? In kindliness, in helpfulness, in service, to those around you? If so, well and good, you have it. If not, then I suspect that what you have been calling love is something else; and you have indeed been greatly fooled. In fact, I am sure it is; for if it does not manifest itself in this way, it cannot be true love, for this is the one grand and never-failing test. Love is the statics, helpfulness and service the dynamics, the former necessary to the latter, but the latter the more powerful, as action is always more powerful than potentiality; and, were it not for the dynamics, the statics might as well not be. Helpfulness, kindliness, service, is but the expression of love. It is love in action; and unless love thus manifests itself in action, it is an indication that it is of that weak and sickly nature that needs exercise, growth, and development, that it may grow and become strong, healthy, vigorous, and true, instead of remaining a little, weak, indefinite, sentimental something or nothing.

It was but yesterday that I heard one of the world's greatest thinkers and speakers, one of our keenest observers of human affairs, state as his opinion that selfishness is the root of all evil. Now, if it is possible for any one thing to be the root of all evil, then I think there is a world of truth in the statement. But, leaving out of account for the present purpose whether it is true or not, it certainly is true that he who can't get beyond self robs his life of its chief charms, and more, defeats the very ends he has in view. It is a well-known law in the natural world about us that whatever hasn't use, that whatever serves no purpose, shrivels up. So it is a law of our own being that he who makes himself of no use, of no service to the great body of mankind, who is concerned only with his own small self, finds that self, small as it is, growing smaller and smaller, and those finer and better and grander qualities of his nature, those that give the chief charm and happiness to life, shrivelling up. Such an one lives, keeps constant company with his own diminutive and stunted self; while he who, forgetting self, makes the object of his life service, helpfulness, and kindliness to others, finds his whole nature growing and expanding, himself becoming large-hearted, magnanimous, kind, loving, sympathetic, joyous, and happy, his life becoming rich and beautiful. For instead of his own little life alone he has entered into and has part in a hundred, a thousand, ay, in countless numbers of other lives; and every success, every joy, every happiness coming to each of these comes as such to him, for he has a part in each and all. And thus it is that one becomes a prince among men, a queen among women.

Why, one of the very fundamental principles of life is, so much love, so much love in return; so much love, so much growth; so much love, so much power; so much love, so much life, – strong, healthy, rich, exulting, and abounding life. The world is beginning to realize the fact that love, instead of being a mere indefinite something, is a vital and living force, the same as electricity is a force, though perhaps of a different nature. The same great fact we are learning in regard to thought, – that thoughts are things, that *thoughts are forces, the most vital and powerful in the universe,* that they have form and substance and power, the quality of the power determined as it is by the quality of the life in whose organism the thoughts are engendered; and so, when a thought is given birth, it does not end there, but takes form, and as a force it goes out and has its effect upon other minds and lives, the effect being determined by its intensity and the quality of the prevailing emotions, and also by the emotions dominating the person at the time the thoughts are engendered and given form.

Science, while demonstrating the great facts it is to-day demonstrating in connection with the mind in its relations to and effects upon the body, is also finding from its very laboratory experiments that each particular kind of thought and emotion has its own peculiar qualities, and hence its own peculiar effects or influences; and these it is classifying with scientific accuracy. A very general classification in just a word would be – those of a higher and those of a lower nature.

Some of the chief ones among those of the lower nature are anger, hatred, jealousy, malice, rage. Their effect, especially when violent, is to emit a poisonous substance into the system, or rather, to set up a corroding influence which transforms the healthy and life-giving secretions of the body into the poisonous and the destructive. When one, for example, is dominated, even if for but a moment by a passion of anger or rage, there is set up in the system what might be justly termed a bodily thunder-storm, which has the effect of souring or corroding the normal and healthy secretions of the body and making them so that instead of life-giving they become poisonous. This, if indulged in to any extent, sooner or later induces the form of disease that this particular state of mind and emotion or passion gives birth to; and it in turn becomes chronic.

We shall ultimately find, as we are beginning to so rapidly to-day, that practically all disease has its origin in perverted mental states or emotions; that anger, hatred, fear, worry, jealousy, lust, as well as all milder forms of perverted mental states and emotions, has each its own peculiar poisoning effects and induces each its own peculiar form of disease, for all life is from within out.

Then some of the chief ones belonging to the other class – mental states and emotions of the higher nature – are love, sympathy, benevolence, kindliness, and good cheer. These are the natural and the normal; and their effect, when habitually entertained, is to stimulate a vital, healthy, bounding, purifying, and life-giving action, the exact opposite of the others; and these very forces, set into a bounding activity, will in time counteract and heal the disease-giving effects of their opposites. Their effects upon the countenance and features in inducing the highest beauty that can dwell there are also marked and all-powerful. So much, then, in regard to the effects of one's thought forces upon the self. A word more in regard to their effects upon others.

Our prevailing thought forces determine the mental atmosphere we create around us, and all who come within its influence are affected in one way or another, according to the quality of that atmosphere; and, though they may not always get the exact thoughts, they nevertheless get the effects of the emotions dominating the originator of the thoughts, and hence the creator of this particular mental atmosphere, and the more sensitively organized the person the more sensitive he or she is to this atmosphere, even at times to getting the exact and very thoughts. So even in this the prophecy is beginning to be fulfilled, – there is nothing hid that shall not be revealed.

If the thought forces sent out by any particular life are those of hatred or jealousy or malice or fault-finding or criticism or scorn, these same thought forces are aroused and sent back from others, so that one is affected not only by reason of the unpleasantness of having such thoughts from others, but they also in turn affect one's own mental states, and through these his own bodily conditions, so that, so far as even the welfare of self is concerned, the indulgence in thoughts and emotions of this nature are most expensive, most detrimental, most destructive.

If, on the other hand, the thought forces sent out be those of love, of sympathy, of kindliness, of cheer and good will, these same forces are aroused and sent back, so that their pleasant, ennobling, warming, and life-giving effects one feels and is influenced by; and so again, so far even as the welfare of self is concerned, there is nothing more desirable, more valuable and life-giving. There comes from others, then, exactly what one sends to and hence calls forth from them.

And would we have all the world love us, we must first then love all the world, – merely a great scientific fact. Why is it that all people instinctively dislike and shun the little, the mean, the self-centred, the selfish, while all the world instinctively, irresistibly, loves and longs for the company of the great-hearted, the tender-hearted, the loving, the magnanimous, the sympathetic, the brave? The mere answer – because – will not satisfy. There is a deep, scientific reason for it, either this or it is not true.

Much has been said, much written, in regard to what some have been pleased to call personal magnetism, but which, as is so commonly true in cases of this kind, is even to-day but little understood. But to my mind personal magnetism in its true sense, and as distinguished from what may be termed a purely animal magnetism, is nothing more nor less than the thought forces sent out by a great-hearted, tender-hearted, magnanimous, loving, sympathetic man or woman; for, let me ask, have you ever known of any great personal magnetism in the case of the little, the mean, the vindictive, the self-centred? Never, I venture to say, but always in the case of the other.

Why, there is nothing that can stand before this wonderful transmuting power of love. So far even as the enemy is concerned, I may not be to blame if I have an enemy; but I am to blame if I keep him as such, especially after I know of this wonderful transmuting power. Have I then an enemy, I will refuse, absolutely refuse, to recognize him as such; and instead of entertaining the thoughts of him that he entertains of me, instead of sending him like thought forces, I will send him only thoughts of love, of sympathy, of brotherly kindness, and magnanimity. But a short time it will be until he feels these, and is influenced by them. Then in addition I will watch my opportunity, and whenever I can, I will even go out of my way to do him some little kindnesses. Before these forces he cannot stand, and by and by I shall find that he who to-day is my bitterest enemy is my warmest friend and it may be my staunchest supporter. No, the wise man is he who by that wonderful alchemy of love transmutes the enemy into the friend, – transmutes the bitterest enemy into the warmest friend and supporter. Certainly this is what the Master meant when he said: "Love your enemies, do good to them that hate you and despitefully use you: thou shalt thereby be heaping coals of fire upon their heads." Ay, thou shalt melt them: before this force they cannot stand. Thou shalt melt them, and transmute them into friends.

> *"You never can tell what your thoughts will do*
> *In bringing you hate or love;*
> *For thoughts are things, and their airy wings*
> *Are swifter than carrier doves.*
> *They follow the law of the universe, –*
> *Each thing must create its kind;*
> *And they speed o'er the track to bring you back*
> *Whatever went out from your mind."*

Yes, science to-day, at the close of this nineteenth century, in the laboratory is discovering and scientifically demonstrating the great, immutable laws upon which the inspired and illuminated ones of all ages have based all their teachings, those who by ordering their lives according to the higher laws of their being get in a moment of time, through the direct touch of inspiration, what it takes the physical investigator a whole lifetime or a series of investigators a series of lifetimes to discover and demonstrate.

PART II

THE APPLICATION

Are you seeking for greatness, O brother of mine,
As the full, fleeting seasons and years glide away?
If seeking directly and for self alone,
The true and abiding you never can stay.
But all self forgetting, know well the law,
It's the hero, and not the self-seeker, who's crowned.
Then go lose your life in the service of others,
And, lo! with rare greatness and glory 'twill abound.

*I*s it your ambition to become great in any particular field, to attain to fame and honor, and thereby to happiness and contentment? Is it your ambition, for example, to become a great *orator,* to move great masses of men, to receive their praise, their plaudits? Then remember that there never has been, there never will, in brief, there never can be a truly great orator without a great *purpose,* a great cause behind him. You may study in all the best schools in the country, the best universities and the best schools of oratory. You may study until you exhaust all these, and then seek the best in other lands. You may study thus until your hair is beginning to change its color, but this of itself will *never* make you a great orator. You may become a demagogue, and, if self-centred, you inevitably will; for this is exactly what a demagogue is, – a great demagogue, if you please, than which it is hard for one to call to mind a more contemptible animal, and the greater the more contemptible. But without laying hold of and building upon this great principle you never can become a great orator.

Call to mind the greatest in the world's history, from Demosthenes – Men of Athens, march against Philip, your country and your fellow-men will be in early bondage unless you give them your best service now – down to our own Phillips and Gough, – Wendell Phillips against the traffic in human blood, John B. Gough against a slavery among his fellow-men more hard and galling and abject than the one just spoken of; for by it the body merely is in bondage, the mind and soul are free, while in this, body, soul, and mind are enslaved. So you can easily discover the great *purpose,* the great cause for *service,* behind each and every one.

The man who can't get beyond himself, his own aggrandizement and interests, must of necessity be small, petty, personal, and at once marks his own limitations; while he whose life is a life of service and self-devotion has no limits, for he thus puts himself at once on the side of the *Universal,* and this more than all else combined gives a tremendous power in oratory. Such a one can mount as on the wings of an eagle, and Nature herself seems to come forth and give a great soul of this kind means and material whereby to accomplish his purposes, whereby the great universal truths go direct to the minds and hearts of his hearers to mould them, to move them; for the orator is he who moulds the minds and hearts of his hearers in the great moulds of universal and eternal truth, and then moves them along a definite line of action, not he who merely speaks pieces to them.

How thoroughly Webster recognized this great principle is admirably shown in that brief but powerful description of eloquence of his; let us pause to listen to a sentence or two: "True eloquence indeed does not consist in speech.... Words and phrases may be marshalled in every way, but they cannot compass it.... Affected passion, intense expression, the pomp of declamation, all may aspire to it; they cannot reach it.... The graces taught in the schools, the costly ornaments and studied contrivances of speech, shock and disgust men when their own lives and the fate of their wives and their children and their country hang on the decision of the hour. Then words have lost their power, rhetoric is vain, and all elaborate oratory contemptible. Even genius itself then feels rebuked and subdued, as in the presence of higher qualities. Then patriotism is eloquent, then self-devotion is eloquent. The clear conception, outrunning the deductions of logic, the high purpose, the firm resolve, the dauntless spirit speaking on the tongue, beaming from the eye, informing every feature and urging the whole man onward, right onward to his object, – this, this is eloquence." And note some of the chief words he has used, – *self-devotion, patriotism, high purpose.* The self-centred man can never know these, and much less can he make use of them.

True, things that one may learn, as the freeing of the bodily agents, the developing of the voice, and so on, that all may become the *true reporters of the soul,* instead of limiting or binding it down, as is so frequently the case in public speakers, – these are all valuable, ay, are very important and very necessary, unless one is content to live below his highest possibilities, and he is wise who recognizes this tact; but these in themselves are but as trifles when compared to those greater, more powerful, and all-essential qualities.

Is it your ambition to become a great *states man?* Note the very first thing, then, the word itself, – *states-man,* a man who gives his life to the service of the State. And do you not recognize the fact that, when one says – a man who gives his life to the service of the State, it is but another way of saying – a man who gives his life to the service of his fellow-men; for what, after all, is any country, any State, in the true sense of the term, but the aggregate, the great body of its individual citizenship. And he who lives for and unto himself, who puts the interests of his own small self before the interests of the thousands, can never become a statesman; for a statesman must be a larger man than this.

Call to your mind the greatest of the world, among those living and among the so-called dead, and you will quickly see that the life of each and every one has been built upon this great principle, and that all have been great and are held as such in just the degree in which it has been. Two of the greatest among Americans, both passed away, would to-day and even more as time goes on, be counted still greater, had they been a little larger in one aspect of their natures, – large enough to have recognized to its fullest extent the eternal truth and importance of this great principle, and had they given the time to the service of their fellow-men that was spent in desiring the Presidency and in all too plainly making it known. Having gained it could have made them no greater, and having so plainly shown their eager and childish desire for it has made them less great. Of the many thousands of men who have been in our American Congress since its beginning, and of the very, very small number comparatively that you are able to call to mind, possibly not over fifty, which would be about one out of every six hundred or more, you will find that you are able to call to mind each one of this very small number on account of his standing for some measure or principle that would to the highest degree increase the human welfare, thus truly fulfilling the great office of a *statesman.*

The one great trouble with our country to-day is that we have but few statesmen. We have a great swarm, a great hoard of politicians; but it is only now and then that we find a man who is large enough truly to deserve the name – statesman. The large majority in public life to-day are there not for the purpose of serving the best interests of those whom they are supposed to represent, but they are there purely for self, purely for self-aggrandizement in this form or in that, as the case may be.

Especially do we find this true in our municipalities. In some, the government instead of being in the hands of those who would make it such in truth, those who would make it serve the interests it is designed to serve, it is in the hands of those who are there purely for self, little whelps, those who will resort to any means to secure their ends, at times even to honorable means, should they seem to serve best the particular purpose in hand. We have but to look around us to see that this is true. The miserable, filthy, and deplorable condition of affairs the Lexow Committee in its investigations not so long ago laid bare to public gaze had its root in what? In the fact that the offices in that great municipality have been and are filled by men who are there to serve in the highest degree the public welfare or by men who are there purely for self-aggrandizement? But let us pass on. This degraded condition of affairs exists not only in this great city, but there are scarcely any that are free from it entirely. Matters are not always to continue thus, however. The American people will learn by and by what they ought fully to realize to-day – that the moment the honest people, the citizens, in distinction from the barnacles, mass themselves and stay massed, the notorious, filthy political rings cannot stand before them for a period of even twenty-four hours. *The right, the good, the true, is all-powerful, and will inevitably conquer sooner or later when brought to the front.* Such is the history of civilization.

Let our public offices – municipal, state, and federal – be filled with men who are in love with the human kind, large men, men whose lives are founded upon this great law of service, and we will then have them filled with statesmen. Never let this glorious word be disgraced, degraded, by applying it to the little, self-centred whelps who are unable to get beyond the politician stage. Then enter public life; but enter it as a man, not as a barnacle: enter it as a statesman, not as a politician.

☙

Is it your ambition to become a great *preacher,* or better yet, with the same meaning, a great *teacher?* Then remember that the greatest of the world have been those who have given themselves in thorough self-devotion and service to their fellow-men, who have given themselves so thoroughly to all they have come in contact with that there has been no room for self. They have not been seekers after fame, or men who have thought so much of their own particular dogmatic ways of thinking as to spend the greater part of their time in discussing dogma, creed, theology, in order, as is so generally true in cases of this kind, to prove that the *ego* you see before you is right in his particular ways of thinking, and that his chief ambition is to have this fact clearly understood, – an abomination, I verily believe, in the sight of God himself, whose children in the mean time are starving, are dying for the bread of life, and an abomination I am sure, in the sight of the great majority of mankind. Let us be thankful, however, for mankind is finding less use for such year by year, and the time will soon come when they will scarcely be tolerated at all.

It is to a very great extent on account of men of this kind, especially in the early history, that the true spirit of religion, of Christianity, has been lost sight of in the mere form. The basket in which it has been deemed necessary to carry it has been held as of greater import than the rare and divinely beautiful fruit itself. The true spirit, that that quickeneth and giveth life and power, has had its place taken by the mere letter, that that alone blighteth and killeth. Instead of running after these finely spun, man-made theories, this stuff, – for stuff is the word, – this that we outgrow once every few years in our march onward and upward, and then stand and laugh as we look back to think that such ideas have ever been held, instead of this, thinking that thus you will gain power, act the part of the wise man, and go each day into the *silence,* there commune with the Infinite, there dwell for a season with the Infinite Spirit of all life, of all power; for you can get *true power* in no other way.

Instead of running about here and there to have your cup filled at these little stagnant pools, dried up as they generally are by the continual rays of a constantly shining egoistic sun, go direct to the great fountain-head, and there drink of the water of life that is poured out freely to every one if he will but go there for it. One can't, however, send and have it brought by another.

Go, then, into the *silence,* even if it be but for a short period, – a period of not more than a quarter or a half-hour a day, – and there come into contact with the Great Source of all life, of all power. *Send out your earnest desires for whatsoever you will; and whatsoever you will, if continually watered by expectation, will sooner or later come to you.* All knowledge, all truth, all power, all wisdom, all things whatsoever, are yours, if you will but go in this way for them. It has been tried times without number, and has never yet once failed where the motives have been high, where the knowledge of the results beforehand has been sufficiently great. Within a fortnight you can know the truth of this for yourself if you will but go in the right way.

All the truly great teachers in the world's history have gotten their powers in this way. You remember the great soul who left us not long ago, he who ministered so faithfully at Trinity, the great preacher of such wonderful powers, the one so truly inspired. It was but an evening or two since, when in conversation with a member of his congregation, we were talking in regard to Phillips Brooks. She was telling of his beautiful and powerful spirit and said that they were all continually conscious of the fact that he had a power they hadn't, but that all longed for; that he seemed to have a great secret of power they hadn't, but that they often tried to find. She continued, and in the very next sentence went on to tell of a fact, – one that I knew full well, – the fact that during a certain period of each day he took himself alone into a little, silent room, he fastened the door behind him, and during this period under no circumstances could he be seen by any one. The dear lady knew these two things, she knew and was influenced by his great soul power, she also knew of his going thus into the silence each day; but, bless her heart, it had never once occurred to her to put the two together.

It is in this way that great soul power is grown; and the men of this great power are the men who move the world, the men who do the great work in the world along all lines, and against whom no man, no power, can stand. Call to mind a number of the world's greatest preachers, or, using again the better term, teachers, and bear in mind I do not mean creed, dogma, form, but religious teachers, – and the one class differs from the other even as the night from the day, – and you will find two great facts in the life of each and all, – great soul power, grown chiefly by much time spent in the silence, and the fact that the life of each has been built upon this one great and all-powerful principle of love, service, and helpfulness for all mankind.

Is it your ambition to become a great *writer?* Very good. But remember that unless you have something to give to the world, something you feel mankind must have, something that will aid them in their march upward and onward, unless you have some service of this kind to render, then you had better be wise, and not take up the pen; for, if your object in writing is merely fame or money, the number of your readers may be exceedingly small, possibly a few score or even a few dozen may be a large estimate.

What an author writes is, after all, the sum total of his life, his habits, his characteristics, his experiences, his purposes. *He never can write more than he himself is.* He can never pass beyond his limitations; and unless he have a purpose higher than writing merely for fame or self-aggrandizement, he thereby marks his own limitations, and what he seeks will never come. While he who writes for the world, because he feels he has something that it needs and that will be a help to mankind, if it *is* something it needs, other things being equal, that which the other man seeks for directly, and so never finds, will come to him in all its fulness. This is the way it comes, and this way only. *Mankind cares nothing for you until you have shown that you care for mankind.*

Note this statement from the letter of a now well-known writer, one whose very first book met with instant success, and that has been followed by others all similarly received. She says, "I never thought of writing until two years and a half ago, when, in order to disburden my mind of certain thoughts that clamored for utterance, I produced," etc. In the light of this we cannot wonder at the remarkable success of her very first and all succeeding books. She had something she felt the world needed and must have; and, with no thought of self, of fame, or of money, she gave it. The world agreed with her; and, as she was large enough to seek for neither, it has given her both.

Note this also: "I write for the love of writing, not for money or reputation. The former I have without exertion, the latter is not worth a pin's point in the general economy of the vast universe. Work done for the love of working brings its own reward far more quickly and surely than work done for mere payment." This is but the formulated statement of what all the world's greatest writers and authors have said or would say, – at least so far as I have come in contact with their opinions in regard to it.

So, unless you are large enough to forget self for the good, for the service of mankind, thus putting yourself on the side of the universal and making it possible for you to give something that will in turn of itself bring fame, you had better be wise, and not lift the pen at all; for what you write will not be taken up, or, if it is, will soon be let fall again.

One of our most charming and most noted American authors says in regard to her writing, "I press my soul upon the white paper"; and let me tell you the reason it in turn makes its impression upon so many thousands of other souls is because hers is so large, so tender, so sympathetic, so loving, that others cannot resist the impression, living as she does not for self, but for the service of others, her own life thus having a part in countless numbers of other lives.

It is only that that comes from the heart that can reach the heart. Take from their shelves the most noted, the greatest works in any library, and you will find that their authors have made them what they are not by a study of the rules and principles of rhetoric, for this of itself never has made and never can make a great writer. They are what they are because the author's very soul has been fired by some great truth or fact that the world has needed, that has been a help to mankind. Large souls they have been, souls in love with all the human kind.

ᴄⱭ

Is it your ambition to become a great *actor?* Then remember that if you make it the object of your life to play to influence the hearts, the lives, and so the destinies of men, this same great law of nature that operates in the case of the orator will come to your assistance, will aid you in your growth and development, and will enable you to attain to heights you could never attain to or even dream of, in case you play for the little *ego* you otherwise would stand for. In the latter case you may succeed in making a third or a fourth rate actor, possibly a second rate; but you can never become one of the world's greatest, and the chances are you may succeed in making not even a livelihood, and thus have your wonderment satisfied why so many who try fail.

In the other case, other things being equal, the height you may attain to is unbounded, depending upon the degree you are able to forget yourself in influencing the minds and the souls, and thus the lives and the destinies of men.

❧

Is it your ambition to become a great *singer?* Then remember that if your thought is only of self, you may never sing at all, unless, indeed, you enjoy singing to yourself, – this, or you will be continually anxious as to the size of your audience. If, on the other hand, you choose this field of work because here you can be of the greatest service to mankind, if your ambition is to sing to the hearts and the lives of men, then this same great law of nature will come to assist you in your growth and development and efforts, and other things being equal, instead of singing to yourself or being anxious as to the size of your audience, you will seldom find time for the first, and your anxiety will be as to whether the place has an audience-chamber large enough to accommodate even a small portion of the people who will seek admittance. You remember Jenny Lind.

❧

Is it your ambition to become a *fashionable society woman,* this and nothing more, intent only upon your own pleasure and satisfaction? Then stop and meditate, if only for a moment; for if this is the case, you never will, ay, you never can find the true and the genuine, for you fail to recognize the great law that there is no such thing as finding true happiness by searching for it *directly,* and the farther on you go the more flimsy and shallow and unsatisfying that imitation you are willing to accept for the genuine will become. You will thereby rob life of its chief charms, defeat the very purpose you have in view. And, while you are at this moment meditating, oh grasp the truth of the great law that you will find your own life only in losing it in the service of others, – that the more of your life you so give, the fuller and the richer, the greater and the grander, the more beautiful and the more happy your own life will become.

And with your abundant means and opportunities build your life upon this great law of service, and experience the pleasure of growing into that full, rich, ever increasing and satisfying life that will result, and that will make you better known, more honored and blessed, than the life of any mere society woman can be, or any life, for that matter; for you are thus living a life the highest this world can know. And you will thus hasten the day when, standing and looking back and seeing the emptiness and the littleness of the other life as compared with this, you will bless the time that your better judgment prevailed and saved you from it. Or, if you chance to be in it already, delay not, but commence now to build upon this true foundation.

Instead of discharging your footman, as did a woman of whom I chance to know, because he finally refused to stand in the rain by the side of her carriage, with his arms folded just so, standing immovable like a mummy (I had almost said like a fool), daring to look neither to one side nor the other, but all the time in the direction of her so-called ladyship, while she spent an hour or two in doing fifteen or twenty minutes' shopping in her desire to make it known that this is Mrs. Q.'s carriage, and this is the footman that goes with it, – instead of doing this, give him an umbrella if necessary, and take him to aid you as you go on your errands of mercy and cheer and service and loving kindness to the innumerable ones all about you who so stand in need of them.

Is there any comparison between the appellation "Lady Bountiful" and "a proud, selfish, pleasure-seeking woman"? And, much more, do you think there is any comparison whatever between the real pleasure and happiness and satisfaction in the lives of the two?

☙

Is it the ambition of your life to *accumulate great wealth,* and thus to acquire a great name, and along with it happiness and satisfaction? Then remember that whether these will come to you will depend *entirely* upon the use and disposition you make of your wealth. If you regard it as a *private trust* to be used for the highest good of mankind, then well and good, these will come to you. If your object, however, is to pile it up, to hoard it, then neither will come; and you will find it a life as unsatisfactory as one can live.

There is, there can be, no greatness in things, in material things, of themselves. The greatness is determined entirely by the use and disposition made of them. The greatest greatness and the only *true* greatness in the world is unselfish love and service and self-devotion to one's fellow-men.

Look at the matter carefully, and tell me candidly if there can be anything more foolish than a man's spending all the days of his life piling up and hoarding money, too mean and too stingy to use any but what is absolutely necessary, accumulating many times more than he can possibly ever use, always eager for more, growing still more eager and grasping the nearer he comes to life's end, then lying down, dying, and leaving it. It seems to me about as sensible for a man to have as the great aim and ambition of life the piling up of an immense pile of old iron in the middle of a large field, and sitting on it day after day because he is so wedded to it that it has become a part of his life and lest a fragment disappear, denying himself and those around him many of the things that go to make life valuable and pleasant, and finally dying there, himself, the soul, so dwarfed and so stunted that he has really a hard time to make his way out of the miserable old body. There is not such a great difference, if you will think of it carefully, – one a pile of old iron, the other a pile of gold or silver, but all belonging to the same general class.

It is a great law of our being that we become like those things we contemplate. If we contemplate those that are true and noble and elevating, we grow in the likeness of these. If we contemplate merely material things, as gold or silver or copper or iron, our souls, our natures, and even our faces become like them, hard and flinty, robbed of their finer and better and grander qualities. Call to mind the person or picture of the miser, and you will quickly see that this is true. Merely nature's great law. He thought he was going to be a master: he finds himself the slave. Instead of possessing his wealth, his wealth possesses him. How often have

I seen persons of nearly or quite this kind! Some can be found almost anywhere. You can call to mind a few, perhaps many.

During the past two or three years two well-known millionaires in the United States, millionaires many times over, have died. The one started into life with the idea of acquiring a great name by accumulating great wealth. These two things he had in mind, – self and great wealth. And, as he went on, he gradually became so that he could see nothing but these. The greed for gain soon made him more and more the slave; and he, knowing nothing other than obedience to his master, piled and accumulated and hoarded, and after spending all his days thus, he then lay down and died, taking not so much as one poor little penny with him, only a soul dwarfed compared to what it otherwise might have been. For it might have been the soul of a royal master instead of that of an abject slave.

The papers noted his death with seldom even a single word of praise. It was regretted by few, and he was mourned by still fewer. And even at his death he was spoken of by thousands in words far from complimentary, all uniting in saying what he might have been and done, what a tremendous power for good, how he might have been loved and honored during his life, and at death mourned and blessed by the entire nation, the entire world. A pitiable sight, indeed, to see a human mind, a human soul, thus voluntarily enslave itself for a few temporary pieces of metal.

The other started into life with the principle that a man's success is to be measured by his *direct usefulness* to his fellow-men, to the world in which he lives, and by this alone; that private wealth is merely a *private trust* to be used for the highest good of mankind. Under the benign influences of this mighty principle of service, we see him great, influential, wealthy; his whole nature expanding, himself growing large-hearted, generous, magnanimous, serving his State, his country, his fellow-men, writing his name on the hearts of all he comes in contact with, so that his name is never thought of by them without feelings of gratitude and praise.

Then as the chief service to his fellow-men, next to his own personal influence and example, he uses his vast fortune, this vast private trust, for the founding and endowing of a great institution of learning, using his splendid business capacities in its organization, having uppermost in mind in its building that young men and young women may there have every advantage at the least possible expense to fit themselves in turn for the greatest *direct usefulness* to their fellow-men while they live in the world.

In the midst of these activities the news comes of his death. Many hearts now are sad. The true, large-hearted, sympathizing friend, the servant of rich and poor alike, has gone away. Countless numbers whom he has befriended, encouraged, helped, and served, bless his name, and give thanks that such a life has been lived. His own great State rises up as his pall-bearers, while the entire nation acts as honorary pall-bearers. Who can estimate the influence of a life such as this? But it cannot be estimated; for it will flow from the ones personally influenced to others, and through them to others throughout eternity. He alone who in His righteous balance weighs each human act can estimate it. And his final munificent gift to mankind will make his name remembered and honored and blessed long after the accumulations of mere plutocrats are scattered and mankind forgets that they have ever lived.

Then have as your object the accumulation of great wealth if you choose; but bear in mind that, unless you are able to get beyond self, it will make you not great, but small, and you will rob life of the finer and better things in it. If, on the other hand, you are guided by the principle that private wealth is but a *private trust,* and that *direct usefulness* or service to mankind is the only real measure of true greatness, and bring your life into harmony with it, then you will become and will be counted great; and with it will come that rich joy and happiness and satisfaction that always accompanies a life of true service, and therefore the best and truest life.

One can never afford to forget that personality, life, and character, that there may be the greatest service, are the chief things, and wealth merely the *incident*. Nor can one afford to be among those who are too mean, too small, or too stingy to invest in anything that will grow and increase these.

PART III

THE UNFOLDMENT

If you'd have a rare growth and unfoldment supreme,
And make life one long joy and contentment complete,
Then with kindliness, love, and good will let it teem,
And with service for all make it fully replete.

If you'd have all the world and all heaven to love you,
And that love with its power would you fully convince,
Then love all the world; and men royal and true,
Will make cry as you pass – "God bless him, the prince!"

ONE beautiful feature of this principle of love and service is that this phase of one's personality, or nature, can be grown. I have heard it asked, If one hasn't it to any marked degree naturally, what is to be done? In reply let it be said, Forget self, get out of it for a little while, and, as it comes in your way, do something for some one, some kind service, some loving favor, it makes no difference how *small* it may appear. But a kind look or word to one weary with care, from whose life all worth living for seems to have gone out; a helping hand or little lift to one almost discouraged, – it may be that this is just the critical moment, a helping hand just now may change a life or a destiny. Show yourself a friend to one who thinks he or she is friendless.

Oh, there are a thousand opportunities each day right where you are, – not the great things far away, but the little things right at hand. With a heart full of love do something: experience the rich returns that will come to you, and it will be unnecessary to urge a repetition or a continuance. The next time it will be easier and more natural, and the next. You know of that wonderful reflex-nerve system you have in your body, – that which says that whenever you do a certain thing in a certain way, it is easier to do the same thing the next time, and the next, and the next, until presently it is done with scarcely any effort on your part at all, it has become your second nature. And thus we have what? Habit. This is the way that all habit is, the way that all habit must be formed. And have you ever fully realized that *life is, after all, merely a series of habits,* and that it lies entirely within one's own power to determine just what that series shall be?

I have seen this great principle made the foundation principle in an institution of learning. It is made not a theory merely as I have seen it here and there, but a vital, living truth. And I wish I had time to tell of its wonderful and beautiful influences upon the life and work of that institution, and upon the lives and the work of those who go out from it. A joy indeed to be there. One can't enter within its walls even for a few moments without feeling its benign influences. One can't go out without taking them with him. I have seen purposes and lives almost or quite transformed; and life so rich, so beautiful, and so valuable opened up, such as the persons never dreamed could be, by being but a single year under these beautiful and life-giving influences.

I have also seen it made the foundation principle of a great summer congress, one that has already done an unprecedented work, one that has a far greater work yet before it, and chiefly by reason of this all-powerful foundation upon which it is built, – conceived and put into operation as it was by a rare and highly illumined soul, one thoroughly filled with the love of service for all the human kind. There are no thoughts of money returns, for everything it has to give is as free as the beautiful atmosphere that pervades it. The result is that there is drawn together, by way of its magnificent corps of lectures as well as those in attendance, a company of people of the rarest type, so that everywhere there is a manifestation of that spirit of love, helpfulness, and kindliness, that permeates the entire atmosphere with a deep feeling of peace, that makes every moment of life a joy.

So enchanting does this spirit make the place that very frequently the single day of some who have come for this length of time has lengthened itself into a week, and the week in turn into a month; and the single week of others has frequently lengthened itself, first into a month, then into the entire summer. There is nothing at all strange in this fact, however; for wherever one finds sweet humanity, he there finds a spot where all people love to dwell.

Making this the fundamental principle of one's life, around which all others properly arrange and subordinate themselves, is not, as a casual observer might think, and as he sometimes suggests, an argument against one's own growth and development, against the highest possible unfoldment of his entire personality and powers. Rather, on the other hand, is it one of the greatest reasons, one of the greatest arguments, in its favor; for, the stronger the personality and the greater the powers, the greater the influence in the service of mankind. If, then, life be thus founded, can there possibly be any greater incentive to that self-development that brings one up to his highest possibilities? A development merely for self alone can never have behind it an incentive, a power so great; *and after all, there is nothing in the world so great, so effective in the service of mankind, as a strong, noble, and beautiful manhood or womanhood.* It is this that in the ultimate determines the influence of every man upon his fellow-men. *Life, character, is the greatest power in the world, and character it is that gives the power; for in all true power, along whatever line it may be, it is after all, living the life that tells.* This is a great law that but few who would have great power and influence seem to recognize, or, at least, that but few seem to act upon.

Are you a writer? You can never write more than you yourself are. Would you write more? Then broaden, deepen, enrich the life. Are you a minister? You can never raise men higher than you have raised yourself. Your words will have exactly the sound of the life whence they come. Hollow the life? Hollow-sounding and empty will be the words, weak, ineffective, false. Would you have them go with greater power, and thus be more effective? Live the life, the power will come. Are you an orator? The power and effectiveness of your words in influencing and moving masses of men depends entirely upon the altitude from which they are spoken. Would you have them more effective, each one filled with a living power? Then elevate the life, the power will come. Are you in the walks of private life? Then, wherever you move, there goes from you, even if there be no word spoken, a silent but effective influence of an elevating or a degrading nature. Is the life high, beautiful? Then the influences are inspiring, life-giving. Is it low, devoid of beauty? The influences then, are disease laden, death-dealing. The tones of your voice, the attitude of your body, the character of your face, all are determined by the life you live, all in turn influence for better or for worse all who come within your radius. And if, as one of earth's great souls has said, the only way truly to help a man is to make him better, then the tremendous power of merely the life itself.

Why, I know personally a young man of splendid qualities and gifts, who was rapidly on the way of ruin, as the term goes, gradually losing control of himself day after day, self-respect almost gone, – already the thought of taking his own life had entered his mind, – who was so inspired with the mere presence and bearing of a royal-hearted young man, one who had complete mastery of himself, and therefore a young man of power, that the very sight of him as he went to and fro in his daily work was a power that called his better self to the front again, awakened the God nature within him, so that he again set his face in the direction of the right, the true, the manly; and to-day there is no grander, stronger, more beautiful soul in all the wide country than he. Yes, there is a powerful influence that resolves itself into a service for all in each individual strong, pure, and noble life.

And have the wonderful possibilities of what may be termed an inner or soul development ever come strongly to your notice? Perhaps not, for as yet only a few have begun to recognize under this name a certain great power that has always existed, – a power that has never as yet been fully understood, and so has been called by this term and by that. It is possible so to develop this soul power that, as we stand merely and talk with a person, there goes out from us a silent influence that the person cannot see or hear, but that he feels, and the influences of which he cannot escape; that, as we merely go into a room in which several persons are sitting, there goes out from us a power, a silent influence that all will feel and will be influenced by, even though not a word be spoken. This has been the power of every man, of every woman, of great and lasting influence in the world's history.

It is just beginning to come to us through a few highly illumined souls that this power can be grown, that it rests upon great natural law that the Author of our being has instituted within us and about us. It is during the next few years that we are to see many wonderful developments along this line; for in this, as in many others, the light is just beginning to break. A few, who are far up on the heights of human development, are just beginning to catch the first few faint flushes of the dawn. Then live to your highest. This of itself will make you of great service to mankind, but without this you never can be. Naught is the difference how hard you may try; and know, even so far as your own highest interests are concerned, that the true joy of existence comes from living to one's highest.

This life, and this alone, will bring that which I believe to be one of the greatest characteristics of a truly great man, – humility; and when one says humility, he necessarily implies simplicity; for the two always go hand in hand. The one is born of the other. The proud, the vain, the haughty, those striving for effect, are never counted among the world's greatest personages. The very fact of one's striving for effect of itself indicates that there is not enough in him to make him really great; while he who really is so needs never concern himself about it, nor does he ever. I can think of no better way for one to attain to humility and simplicity than for him to have his mind off of self in the service of others. Vanity, that most dangerous quality, and especially for young people, is the outcome of one's always regarding self.

Mrs. Henry Ward Beecher once said that, when they lived in the part of Brooklyn known as the Heights, they could always tell when Mr. Beecher was coming in the evening from the voices and the joyous laughter of the children. All the street urchins, as well as the more well-to-do children in the vicinity, knew him, and would often wait for his coming. When they saw him in the distance, they would run and gather around him, get hold of his hands, into those large overcoat pockets for the nuts and the good things he so often filled them with before starting for home, knowing as he did full well what was coming, tug at him to keep him with them as long as they could, he all the time laughing or running as if to get away, never too great – ay, rather let us say, great enough – to join with them in their sports.

That mysterious dignity of a man less great, therefore with less of humility and simplicity, with mind always intent upon self and his own standing, would have told him that possibly this might not be just the "proper thing" to do. But even the children, street urchins as well as those well-to-do, found in this great loving soul a friend. Recall similar incidents in the almost daily life of Lincoln and in the lives of all truly great men. All have that beautiful and ever-powerful characteristic, that simple, childlike nature.

Another most beautiful and valuable feature of this life is its effect upon one's own growth and development. There is a law which says that one can't do a kind act or a loving service for another without its bringing rich returns to his own life and growth. This is an invariable law. Can I then, do a kind act or a loving service for a brother or a sister, – and all indeed are such because children of the same Father, – why, I should be glad – ay, doubly glad of the opportunity. If I do it thus out of love, forgetful of self, for aught I know it may do me more good than the one I do it for, in its influence upon the growing of that rich, beautiful, and happy life it is mine to grow; though the joy and satisfaction resulting from it, the highest, the sweetest, the keenest this life can know, are of themselves abundant rewards.

In addition to all this it scarcely ever fails that those who are thus aided by some loving service may be in a position somehow, some-when, somewhere, either directly or indirectly, and at a time when it may be most needed or most highly appreciated, to do in turn a kind service for him who, with never a thought of any possible return, has dealt kindly with them. So

"Cast your bread upon the waters, far and wide your treasures strew,
Scatter it with willing fingers, shout for joy to see it go!
You may think it lost forever; but, as sure as God is true,
In this life and in the other it will yet return to you."

Have you sorrows or trials that seem very heavy to bear? Then let me tell you that one of the best ways in the world to lighten and sweeten them is to lose yourself in the service of others, in helping to bear and lighten those of a fellow-being whose, perchance, are much more grievous than your own. It is a great law of your being which says you can do this. Try it, and experience the truth for yourself, and know that, when turned in this way, sorrow is the most beautiful soul-refiner of which the world knows, and hence not to be shunned, but to be welcomed and rightly turned.

There comes to my mind a poor widow woman whose life would seem to have nothing in it to make it happy, but, on the other hand, cheerless and tiresome, and whose work would have been very hard, had it not been for a little crippled child she dearly loved and cared for, and who was all the more precious to her on account of its helplessness. Losing herself and forgetting her own hard lot in the care of the little cripple, her whole life was made cheerful and happy, and her work not hard, but easy, because lightened by love and service for another. And this is but one of innumerable cases of this kind.

So you may turn your sorrows, you may lighten your burdens, by helping bear the burdens, if not of a crippled child, then of a brother or a sister who in another sense may be crippled, or who may become so but for your timely service. You can find them all about you: never pass one by.

By building upon this principle, the poor may thus live as grandly and as happily as the rich, those in humble and lowly walks of life as grandly and as happily as those in what seem to be more exalted stations. Recognizing the truth, as we certainly must by this time, that one is *truly* great only in so far as this is made the fundamental principle of his life, it becomes evident that that longing for greatness for its and for one's own sake falls away, and none but a diseased mind cares for it; for no sooner is it grasped than, as a bubble, it bursts, because it is not the true, the permanent, but the false, the transient. On the other hand, he who forgetting self and this kind of greatness, falsely so called, in the service of his fellow-men, by this very fact puts himself on the right track, the only track for the true, the genuine; and in what degree it will come to him depends entirely upon his adherence to the law.

And do you know the influence of this life in the moulding of the features, that it gives the highest beauty that can dwell there, the beauty that comes from within, – the *soul beauty,* so often found in the paintings of the old masters. *True beauty must come, must be grown, from, within.* That outward veneering, which is so prevalent, can never be even a poor imitation of this type of the true, the genuine. To appreciate fully the truth of this, it is but necessary to look for a moment at that beautiful picture by Sant, the "Soul's Awakening," a face that grows more beautiful each time one looks at it, and that one never tires of looking at, and compare with it the fractional parts of apothecary shops we see now and then – or so often, to speak more truly – on the streets. A face of this higher type carries with it a benediction wherever it goes.

A beautiful little incident came to my notice not long ago. It was a very hot and dusty day. The passengers on the train were weary and tired. The time seemed long and the journey cheerless. A lady with a face that carries a benediction to all who see her entered the car with a little girl, also of that type of beauty that comes from within, and with a voice musical, sweet, and sparkling, such as also comes from this source.

The child, when they were seated, had no sooner spoken a few words before she began to enlist the attention of her fellow-passengers. She began playing peek-a-boo with a staid and dignified old gentleman in the seat behind her. He at first looked at her over his spectacles, then lowered his paper a little, then a little more, and a little more. Finally, he dropped it altogether, and, apparently forgetting himself and his surroundings, became oblivious to everything in the fascinating pleasure he was having with the little girl. The other passengers soon found themselves following his example. All papers and books were dropped. The younger folks gave way to joyous laughter, and all seemed to vie with each other in having the honor of receiving a word or a smile from the little one.

The dust, the heat, the tired, cheerless feelings were all forgotten; and when these two left the car, the little girl waving them good-by, instinctively, as one person, all the passengers waved it to her in return, and two otherwise dignified gentlemen, leaving their seats, passed over to the other side, and looked out of the window to see her as long as they could. Something as an electrical spark seemed to have passed through the car. All were light-hearted and happy now; and the conditions in the car, compared to what they were before these two entered, would rival the work of the stereopticon, so far as completeness of change is concerned. You have seen such faces and have heard such voices. They result from a life the kind we are considering. They are but its outward manifestations, spontaneous as the water from the earth as it bursts forth a natural fountain.

We must not fail also to notice the effect of this life upon one's manners and bearing. True politeness comes from a life founded upon this great principle, and from this alone. This gives the true gentleman, – *gentle-man*, – a man gentle, kind, loving, courteous from nature. Such a one can't have anything but true politeness, can't be anything but a gentle-man; for one can't truly be anything but himself. So the one always intent upon and thinking of self cannot be the true gentleman, notwithstanding the artful contrivances and studied efforts to appear so, but which so generally reveal his own shallowness and artificiality, and disgust all with whom he comes in contact.

I sometimes meet a person who, when introduced, will go through a series of stiff, cold, and angular movements, the knee at such a bend, the foot at such an angle, the back with such a bend or hump, – much less pleasant to see than that of a camel or a dromedary, for with these it is natural, – so that I have found myself almost thinking, Poor fellow, I wonder what the trouble is, whether he will get over it all right. It is so very evident that he all the time has his mind upon himself, wondering whether or not he is getting everything just right. What a relief to turn from such a one to one who, instead of thinking always of self, has continually in mind the ease and comfort and pleasure he can give to others, who, in other words, is the true *gentle-man,* and with whom true politeness is natural; for one's every act is born of his thoughts.

It is said that there was no truer gentleman in all Scotland than Robert Burns. And yet he was a farmer all his life, and had never been away from his native little rural village into a city until near the close of his life, when, taking the manuscripts that for some time had been accumulating in the drawer of his writing-table up to Edinburgh, he captivated the hearts of all in the capital. Without studied contrivances, he was the true gentleman, and true politeness was his, because his life was founded upon the principle that continually brought from his pen lines such as: –

> *"It's coming yet, for a' that,*
> *That man to man, the warld o'er,*
> *Shall brothers be for a' that!"*

And under the influence of this principle, he was a gentleman by nature, and one of nature's noblemen, without ever thinking whether he was or not, as he who is truly such never needs to and never does.

And then recall the large-hearted Ben Franklin, when sent to the French court. In his plain gray clothes, unassuming and entirely forgetful of himself, how he captured the hearts of all, of even the giddy society ladies, and how he became and remained while there the centre of attraction in that gay capital! His politeness, his manners, all the result of that great, kind, loving, and helpful nature which made others feel that it was they he was devoting himself to and not himself.

This little extract from a letter written by Franklin to George Whitefield will show how he regarded the great principle we are considering: "As to the kindness you mention, I wish it could have been of more service to you. But, if it had, the only thanks I should desire is that you would always be equally ready to serve any other person that may need your assistance; and so let good offices go around, for mankind are all of a family. For my own part, when I am employed in serving others, I do not look upon myself as conferring favors, but as paying debts. In my travels, and since my settlement, I have received much kindness from men to whom I shall never have any opportunity of making any direct return, and numberless mercies from God, who is infinitely above being benefited by our services. These kindnesses from men I can, therefore, only return on their fellow-men; and I can only show my gratitude for these mercies from God by a readiness to help his other children and my brethren."

No, true gentlemanliness and politeness always comes from within, and is born of a life of love, kindliness, and service. This is the universal language, known and understood everywhere, even when our words are not. There is, you know, a beautiful old proverb which says, "He who is kind and courteous to strangers thereby shows himself a citizen of the world." And there is nothing so remembered, and that so endears one to all mankind, as this universal language. Even dumb animals understand it and are affected by it. How quickly the dog, for example, knows and makes it known when he is spoken to and treated kindly or the reverse! And here shall not a word be spoken in connection with that great body of our fellow-creatures whom, because we do not understand their language, we are accustomed to call dumb? The attitude we have assumed toward these fellow-creatures, and the treatment they have been subjected to in the past, is something almost appalling.

There are a number of reasons why this has been true. Has not one been on account of a belief in a future life for man, but not for the animal? A few years ago a gentleman left by will some fifty thousand dollars for the work of Henry Bergh's New York Society. His relatives contested the will on the ground of insanity, – on the ground of insanity because he believed in a future life for animals. The judge, in giving his decision sustaining the will, stated that after a very careful investigation, he found that fully half the world shared the same belief. Agassiz thoroughly believed it. An English writer has recently compiled a list of over one hundred and seventy English authors who have so thoroughly believed it as to write upon the subject. The same belief has been shared by many of the greatest thinkers in all parts of the world, and it is a belief that is constantly gaining ground.

Another and perhaps the chief cause has been on account of a supposed inferior degree of intelligence on the part of animals, which in another form would mean, that they are less able to care for and protect themselves. Should this, however, be a reason why they should be neglected and cruelly treated? Nay, on the other hand, should this not be the greatest reason why we should all the more zealously care for, protect, and kindly treat them?

You or I may have a brother or a sister who is not normally endowed as to brain power, who, perchance, may be idiotic or insane, or who, through sickness or mishap, is weakminded; but do we make this an excuse for neglecting, cruelly treating, or failing to love such a one? On the contrary, the very fact that he or she is not so able to plan for, care for, and protect him or her self, is all the greater reason for all the more careful exercise of these functions on our part. But, certainly, there are many animals around us with far more intelligence, at least manifested intelligence, than this brother or sister. The parallel holds, but the absurd falsity of the position we assume is most apparent. No truer nobility of character can anywhere manifest itself than is shown in one's attitude toward and treatment of those weaker or the so-called inferior, and so with less power to care for and protect themselves. Moreover, I think we shall find that we are many times mistaken in regard to our beliefs in connection with the inferior intelligence of at least many animals. If, instead of using them simply to serve our own selfish ends without a just recompense, without a thought further than as to what we can get out of them, and then many times casting them off when broken or of no further service, and many times looking down upon, neglecting, or even abusing them, – if, instead of this, we would deal equitably with them, love them, train and educate them the same as we do our children, we would be somewhat surprised at the remarkable degree of intelligence the "dumb brutes" possess, and also the remarkable degree of training they are capable of. What, however, can be expected of them when we take the attitude we at present hold toward them?

Page after page might readily be filled with most interesting as well as inspiring portrayals of their superior intelligence, their remarkable capabilities under kind and judicious training, their *faithfulness* and *devotion*. The efforts of such noble and devoted workers as Henry Bergh in New York, of George T. Angell in Massachusetts, and many others in various parts of the country, have already brought about a great change in our attitude toward and relations with this great body of our fellow-creatures, and have made all the world more thoughtful, considerate, and kind. This, however, is just the beginning of a work that is assuming greater and ever greater proportions.

The work of the American Humane Education Society[1] is probably surpassed in its vitality and far-reaching results by the work of no other society in the world to-day. Its chief object is the humane education of the American people; and through one phase of its work alone – its Bands of Mercy, over twenty-five thousand of which have already been formed, giving regular, systematic humane training and instruction to between one and two million children, and these continually increasing in numbers – a most vital work is being done, such as no man can estimate.

The humane sentiment inculcated in one's relations with the animal world, and its resultant feelings of sympathy, tenderness, love, and care, will inevitably manifest itself in one's relations with his fellows; and I for one, would rejoice to see this work carried into every school throughout the length and breadth of the land. In many cases this one phase of the child's training would be of far more vital value and import as he grows to manhood than all the rest of the schooling combined, and it would form a most vital entering wedge in the solution of our social situation.

And why should we not speak to and kindly greet an animal as we pass it, as instinctively as we do a human fellow-being? Though it may not get our words, it will invariably get the attitude and the motive that prompts them, and will be affected accordingly. This it will do every time. Animals in general are marvellously sensitive to the mental conditions, the thought forces, and emotions of people. Some are peculiarly sensitive, and can detect them far more quickly and unerringly than many people can.

---

1   Headquarters at Boston, Mass.

It ought to help us greatly in our relations with them ever fully to realize that they with us are parts of the one Universal Life, simply different forms of the manifestation of the One Life, having their part to play in the economy of the great universe the same as we have ours, having their destiny to work out the same as we have ours, and just as important, just as valuable, in the sight of the All in All as we ourselves.

> "I saw deep in the eyes of the animals the human soul look out upon me.

> "I saw where it was born deep down under feathers and fur, or condemned for a while to roam four-footed among the brambles. I caught the clinging mute glance of the prisoner, and swore I would be faithful.

> "Thee my brother and sister I see, and mistake not. Do not be afraid. Dwelling thus for a while, fulfilling thy appointed time, thou, too, shall come to thyself at last.

> "Thy half-warm horns and long tongue lapping round my wrist do not conceal thy humanity any more than the learned talk of the pedant conceals his, – for all thou art dumb, we have words and plenty between us.

> "Come nigh, little bird, with your half-stretched quivering wings, – within you I behold choirs of angels, and the Lord himself in vista."[2]

But a small thing, apparently, is a kind look, word, or service of some kind; but, oh! who can tell where it may end? It costs the giver comparatively nothing; but who can tell the priceless value to him who receives it? The cup of loving service, be it merely a cup of cold water, may grow and swell into a boundless river, refreshing and carrying life and hope in turn to numberless others, and these to others, and so have no end. This may be just the critical moment in some life. Given now, it may save or change a life or a destiny. So don't withhold the bread that's in your keeping, but

"Scatter it with willing fingers, shout for joy to see it go."

There is no greater thing in life that you can do, and nothing that will bring you such rich and precious returns.

---

2   Toward Democracy.

The question is sometimes asked, How can one feel a deep and genuine love, a love sufficient to manifest itself in service for all? – there are some so mean, so small, with so many peculiar, objectionable, or even obnoxious characteristics. True, very true, apparently at least; but another great law of life is that *we find in men and women exactly those qualities, those characteristics, we look for, or that are nearest akin to the predominant qualities or characteristics of our own natures.* If we look for the peculiar, the little, the objectionable, these we shall find; but back of all this, all that is most apparent on the exterior, in the depths of each and every human soul, is the good, the true, the brave, the loving, the divine, the God-like, that that never changes, the very God Himself that at some time or another will show forth His full likeness.

And still another law of life is that others usually manifest to us that which our own natures, or, in other words, our own thoughts and emotions, call forth. The same person, for example, will come to two different people in an entirely different way, because the larger, better, purer, and more universal nature of the one calls forth the best, the noblest, the truest in him; while the smaller, critical, personal nature of the other calls forth the opposite. The wise man is therefore careful in regard to what he has to say concerning this or that one; for, generally speaking, it is a sad commentary upon one's self if he find only the disagreeable, the objectionable. *One lives always in the atmosphere of his own creation.*

Again, it is sometimes said, But such a one has such and such habits or has done so and so, has committed such and such an error or such and such a crime. But who, let it be asked, constituted me a judge of my fellow-man? Do I not recognize the fact that the moment I judge my fellow-man, by that very act I judge myself? One of two things, I either judge myself or hypocritically profess that never once in my entire life have I committed a sin, an error of any kind, never have I stumbled, never fallen, and by that very profession I pronounce myself at once either a fool or a knave, or both.

Again, it is said, But even for the sake of helping, of doing some service, I could not for my own sake, for character's, for reputation's sake, I could not afford even to be seen with such a one. What would people, what would my friends, think and say? True, apparently at least, but, if my life, my character, has such a foundation, a foundation so weak, so uncertain, so tottering, as to be affected by anything of this kind, I had better then look well to it, and quietly, quickly, but securely, begin to rebuild it; and, when I am sure that it is upon the true, deep, substantial foundation, the only additional thing then necessary is for me to reach that glorious stage of development which quickly gets one out of the personal into the universal, or rather that indicates that he is already out of the one and into the other, when he can say: They think. What do they think? Let them think. They say. What do they say? Let them say.

And, then, the supreme charity one should have, when he realizes the fact that *the great bulk of the sin and error in the world is committed not through choice, but through ignorance.* Not that the person does not know many times that this or that course of action is wrong, that it is wrong to commit this error or sin or crime; but the ignorance comes in his belief that in this course of conduct he is deriving pleasure and happiness, and his ignorance of the fact that through a different course of conduct he would derive a pleasure, a happiness, much keener, higher, more satisfying and enduring.

Never should we forget that we are all the same in motive, – pleasure and happiness: we differ only in method; and this difference in method is solely by reason of some souls being at any particular time more fully evolved, and thus having a greater knowledge of the great, immutable laws under which we live, and by putting the life into more and ever more complete harmony with these higher laws and forces, and in this way bringing about the highest, the keenest, the most abiding pleasure and happiness instead of seeking it on the lower planes.

While all are the same in essence, all a part of the One Infinite, Eternal, all with the same latent possibilities, all reaching ultimately the same place, it nevertheless is true that at any particular time some are more fully awakened, evolved, unfolded. One should also be careful, if life is continuous, eternal, how he judges any particular life merely from these threescore years and ten; for the very fact of life, in whatever form, means continual activity, growth, advancement, unfoldment, attainment, and, if there is the one, there must of necessity be the other. So in regard to this one or that one, no fears need be entertained.

By the door of my woodland cabin stood during the summer a magnificent tube-rose stock. The day was when it was just putting into bloom; and then I counted buds – latent flowers – to the number of over a score. Some eight or ten one morning were in full bloom. The ones nearer the top did not bloom forth until some two and three weeks later, and for some it took quite a month to reach the fully perfected stage. These certainly were not so beautiful, so satisfying, as those already in the perfect bloom, those that had already reached their highest perfection. But should they on this account be despised? Wait, wait and give the element of time an opportunity of doing its work; and you may find that by and by, when these have reached their highest perfection, they may even far transcend in beauty and in fragrance those at present so beautiful, so fragrant, so satisfying, those that we so much admire.

Here we recognize the element of time. How foolish, how childish, how puerile, to fail or even refuse to do the same when it comes to the human soul, with all its God-like possibilities! And, again, how foolish, because some of the blooms on the rose stock had not reached their perfection as soon as others, to have pronounced them of no value, unworthy, and to have refused them the dews, the warm rains, the life-giving sunshine, the very agencies that hastened their perfected growth! Yet this puerile, unbalanced attitude is that taken by untold numbers in the world to-day toward many human souls on account of their less mature unfoldment at any given time.

Why, the very fact that a fellow-man and a brother has this or that fault, error, undesirable or objectionable characteristic, is of itself the very reason he needs all the more of charity, of love, of kindly help and aid, than is needed by the one more fully developed, and hence more free from these. All the more reason is there why the best in him should be recognized and ever called to the front.

The wise man is he who, when he desires to rid a room of darkness or gloom, does not attempt to drive it out directly, but who throws open the doors and the windows, that the room may be flooded with the golden sunlight; for in its presence darkness and gloom cannot remain. So the way to help a fellow-man and a brother to the higher and better life is not by ever prating upon and holding up to view his errors, his faults, his shortcomings, any more than in the case of children, but by recognizing and ever calling forth the higher, the nobler, the divine, the God-like, *by opening the doors and the windows of his own soul,* and thus bringing about a spiritual perception, that he may the more carefully listen to the inner voice, that he may the more carefully follow "the light that lighteth every man that cometh into the world." For in the exact proportion that the interior perception comes will the outer life and conduct accord with it, – so far, and no farther.

Where in all the world's history is to be found a more beautiful or valuable incident than this? A group of men, self-centred, self-assertive, have found a poor woman who, in her blindness and weakness, has committed an error, the same one that they, in all probability, have committed not once, but many times; *for the rule is that they are first to condemn who are-most at fault themselves.* They bring her to the Master, they tell him that she has committed a sin, – ay, more, that she has been taken in the very act, – and ask what shall be done with her, informing him that, in accordance with the olden laws, such a one should be stoned.

But, quicker than thought, that great incarnation of spiritual power and insight reads their motives; and, after allowing them to give full expression to their accusations, he turns, and calmly says, "He among you that is *without sin,* let *him* cast the first stone." So saying, he stoops down, as if he is writing in the sand. The accusers, feeling the keen and just rebuke, in the mean time sneak out, until not one remains. The Master, after all have gone, turns to the woman, his sister, and kindly and gently says, "And where are thine accusers? doth no man condemn thee?" "No man, Lord." *"And neither do I condemn thee: go thou, and sin no more."* Oh, the beauty, the soul pathos! Oh, the royal-hearted brother! Oh, the invaluable lesson to us all!

I have no doubt that this gentle, loving admonition, this calling of the higher and the better to the front, set into operation in her interior nature forces that hastened her progress from the purely animal, the unsatisfying, the diminishing, to the higher spiritual, the satisfying, the ever-increasing, or, even more, that made it instantaneous, but that in either case brought about the new birth, – the new birth that comes with the awakening of the soul out of its purely physical sense-life to the higher spiritual perception and knowledge of itself, and thus the birth of the higher out of the lower, as at some time or another comes to each and every human soul.

And still another fact that should make us most charitable toward and slow to judge, or rather refuse to judge, a fellow-man and a brother, – the fact that we cannot know the intense strugglings and fightings he or she may be subjected to, though accompanied, it is true, by numerous stumblings and fallings, though the latter we see, while the former we fail to recognize. Did we, however, know the truth of the matter, it may be that in the case of ourselves, who are so quick to judge, had we the same temptations and fightings, the battle would not be half so nobly, so manfully fought, and our stumblings and fallings might be many times the number of his or of hers. Had we infinite knowledge and wisdom, our judgments would be correct; though, had we infinite knowledge and wisdom, we would be spared the task, though perhaps pleasure would seem to be the truer word to use, of our own self-imposed judgments.

Even so, then, if I cannot give myself in thorough love and service and self-devotion to each and all of the Father's other children, to every brother, no matter what the rank, station, or apparent condition, it shows that at least one of several things is radically wrong with self; and it also indicates that I shall never know the full and supreme joy of existence until I am able to and until I regard each case in the light of a rare and golden opportunity, in which I take a supreme delight.

Although what has just been said is true, at the same time there are occasions when it must be taken with wise discretion; and, although there are things it may be right for me to do for the sake of helping another life, at the same time there are things it may be unwise for me to do. I have sympathy for a friend who is lying in the gutter; but it would be very unwise for me to get myself into the same condition, and go and lie with him, thinking that only thus I could show my fullest sympathy, and be of greatest help to him. On the contrary, it is only as I stand on the higher ground that I am able to reach forth the hand that will truly lift him up. The moment I sink myself to the same level, my power to help ceases.

Just as unwise, to use a familiar example, far more unwise, would it be for me, were I a woman, to think of marrying a man who is a drunkard or a libertine, thinking that because I may love him I shall be able to reform him. In the first place, I should find that the desired results could not be accomplished in this way, or rather, no results that could not be accomplished, and far more readily accomplished otherwise, and at far less expense. In the second place, I could not afford to subject myself to the demands, the influences, of one such, and so either sink myself to his level or, if not, then be compelled to use the greater part of my time, thought, and energy in demonstrating over existing conditions, and keeping myself true to the higher life, the same time that might be used in helping the lives of many others. If I sink myself to his level, I do not help, but aid all the more in dragging him down, or, if I do not sink to his level, then in the degree that I approach it do I lose my power over and influence with that life. Especially would it be unwise on my part if on his part there is no real desire for a different course, and no manifest endeavor to attain to it. Many times it seems necessary for such a one to wallow in the deepest of the mire, until, to use a commonplace phrase, he has his fill. He will then be ready to come out, will then be open to influence. I in the mean time, instead of entering into the mire with him, instead of subjecting my life to his influences, will stand up on the higher ground, and will ever point him upward, will ever reach forth a hand to help him upward, and will thus subject *him* to the higher influences; and, by preserving myself in this attitude, I can do the same for many other lives. In it all there will be no bitterness, no condemnation, no casting off, but the highest charity, sympathy and love; and it is only by this method that I can manifest the highest, only by this method that I can the most truly aid, for only as I am lifted up can I draw others unto me.

In this matter of service, as in all other matters, that supreme regulator of human life and conduct – good common sense – must always be used. There are some natures, for example, whom the more we would do for, the more we would have to do for, who, in other words, would become dependent, losing their sense of self-dependence. For such the highest service one can render is as judiciously and as indirectly as possible to lead them to the sense of self-reliance. Then there are others whose natures are such that, the more they are helped, the more they expect, the more they demand, even as their right, who, in other words, are parasites or vultures of the human kind. In this case, again, the greatest service that can be rendered may be a refusal of service, a refusal of aid in the ordinary or rather expected forms, and a still greater service in the form of teaching them that great principle of justice, of compensation, that runs through all the universe, – that for every service there must be in some form or another an adequate service in return, that the law of compensation in one form or another is absolute, and, in fact, the greatest forms of service we can render any one are, generally speaking, along the lines of teaching him the great laws of his own being, the great laws of his true possibilities and powers and so the great laws of self-help.

And, again, it is possible for one whose heart goes out in love and service for all, and who, by virtue of lacking that long range of vision or by virtue of not having a grasp of things in their entirety or wholeness, may have his time, his energies so dissipated in what seems to be the highest service that he is continually kept from his own highest unfoldment, powers, and possessions, the very things that in their completeness would make him a thousand-fold more effective and powerful in his own life, and hence in the life of real service and influence. And, in a case of this kind, many times the mark of the most absolute unselfishness is a strong and marked selfishness, which will prove however to be a selfishness only in the seeming.

The self should never be lost sight of. It is the one thing of supreme importance, the greatest factor even in the life of the greatest service. Being always and necessarily precedes doing: having always and necessarily precedes giving. But this law also holds: that when there is the being, it is all the more increased by the doing; when there is the having, it is all the more increased by the giving. *Keeping to one's self dwarfs and stultifies. Hoarding brings loss: using brings even greater gain.* In brief, the more we are, the more we can do; the more we have, the more we can give.

The most truly successful, the most powerful and valuable life, then, is the life that is first founded upon this great, immutable law of love and service, and that then becomes supremely self-centred, – supremely self-centred that it may become all the more supremely unself-centred; in other words, the life that looks v/ell to self, that there may be the ever greater self, in order that there may be the ever greater service.

PART IV

THE AWAKENING

If you'd live a religion that's noble,
That's God-like and true,
A religion the grandest that men
Or that angels can,
Then live, live the truth
Of the brother who taught you,
It's love to God, service and love
To the fellow-man.

SOCIAL problems are to be among the greatest problems of the generation just moving on to the stage of action. They, above all others, will claim the attention of mankind, as they are already claiming it across the waters even as at home. The attitude of the two classes toward each other, or the separation of the classes, will be by far the chief problem of them all. Already it is imperatively demanding a solution. Gradually, as the years have passed, this separation has been going on, but never so rapidly as of late. Each has come to regard the other as an enemy, with no interests in common, but rather that what is for the interests of the one must necessarily be to the detriment of the other.

The great masses of the people, the working classes, those who as much, if not more than many others ought to be there, are not in our churches to-day. They already feel that they are not wanted there, and that the Church even is getting to be their enemy. There must be a reason for this, for it is impossible to have an effect without its preceding cause. It is indeed time to waken up to these facts and conditions; for they must be *squarely* met. A solution is imperatively demanded, and the sooner it comes, the better; for, if allowed to continue thus, all will come back to be paid for, intensified a thousand-fold, – ay, to be paid for even by many innocent ones.

Let this great principle of service, helpfulness, love, and self-devotion to the interests of one's fellow-men be made the fundamental principle of all lives, and see how simplified these great and all-important questions will become. Indeed, they will almost solve themselves. It is the man all for self, so small and so short sighted that he can't get beyond his own selfish interests, that has done more to bring about this state of affairs than all other causes combined. Let the cause be removed, and then note the results.

For many years it has been a teaching even of political economy that an employer buys his help just as he buys his raw material or any other commodity; and this done, he is in no way responsible for the welfare of those he employs. In fact, the time isn't so far distant when the employed were herded together as animals, and were treated very much as such. But, thanks be to God, a better and a brighter day is dawning. Even the employer is beginning to see that practical ethics, or true Christianity, and business cannot and must not be divorced; that the man he employs, instead of being a mere animal whose services he buys, is, after all his fellow-man and his brother, and demands a treatment as such, and that when he fails to recognize this truth, a righteous God steps in, demanding a penalty for its violation.

He is recognizing the fact that whatsoever is for the well-being of the one he employs, that whatever privileges he is enabled to enjoy that will tend to grow and develop his physical, his mental, and his moral life, that will give him an agreeable home and pleasant family relations, that whatever influences tend to elevate him and to make his life more happy, are a direct gain, even from a financial standpoint for himself, by its increasing for him the efficiency of the man's labor. It is already recognized as a fact that the employer who interests himself in these things, other things being equal, is the most successful. Thus the old and the false are breaking away before the right and the true, as all inevitably must sooner or later; and the divinity and the power of the workingman is being ever more fully recognized.

In the very remote history of the race there was one who, violating a great law, having wronged a brother, asked, "Am I my brother's keeper?" Knowing that he was, he nevertheless deceitfully put the question in this way in his desire, if possible, to avoid the responsibility. Many employers in their selfishness and greed for gain have asked this same question in this same way. They have thought they could thus defeat the sure and eternal laws of a Just Ruler, but have thereby deceived themselves the more. These more than any others have to a great degree brought about the present state of affairs in the industrial and social world.

Just as soon as the employer recognizes the falsity of these old teachings and practices, and the fact that he cannot buy his employee's services the same as he buys his raw material, with no further responsibility, but that the two are on vastly different planes, that his employee is his fellow-man and his brother, and that he is his brother's keeper, and will be held responsible as such, that it is to his own highest interests, as well as to the highest interests of those he employs and to society in general, to recognize this; and just as soon as he who is employed fully appreciates his opportunities and makes the highest use of all, and in turn takes an active, personal interest in all that pertains to his employer's welfare, – just that soon will a solution of this great question come forth, and no sooner.

It is not so much a question of legislation as of education and right doing, thus a dealing with the *individual,* and so a prevention and a cure, not merely a suppression and a regulation, which is always sure to fail; for, in a case of right or wrong no question is ever settled finally until it is settled rightly.

The individual, dealing with the individual is necessarily at the bottom of all true social progress. There can't be anything worthy the name without it. The truth will at once be recognized by all *that the good of the whole defends upon the good of each, and the good of each makes the good of the whole.* Attend, then, to the individual, and the whole will take care of itself. Let each individual work in harmony with every other, and harmony will pervade the whole. The old theory of competition – that in order to have great advancement, great progress, we must have great competition to induce it – is as false as it is savage and detrimental in its nature. We are just reaching that point where the larger men and women are beginning to see its falsity. They are recognizing the fact that, *not competition, but co-operation, reciprocity, is the great, the true power,* – to climb, not by attempting to drag, to keep down one's fellows, but by aiding them, and being in turn aided by them, thus combining, and so multiplying the power of all instead of wasting a large part one against the other.

And grant that a portion do succeed in rising, while the other portion remain in the lower condition, it is of but little value so far as their own peace and welfare are concerned; for they can never be what they would be, were all up together. Each is but a part, a member, of the great civil body; and no member, let alone the entire body, can be perfectly well, perfectly at ease, when any other part is in dis-ease. No one part of the community, no one part of the nation, can stand alone: all are dependent, interdependent. This is the uniform teaching of history from the remotest times in the past right through to the present. A most admirable illustration of this fact – if indeed the word "admirable" can be used in connection with a matter so deplorable – was the unparalleled labor trouble we had in our great Western city but a few summers ago. The wise man is he who learns from experiences of this terrific nature.

No, not until this all-powerful principle is fully recognized, and is built upon so thoroughly that the brotherhood principle, the principle of oneness can enter in, and each one recognizes the fact that his own interests and welfare depend upon the interests, the welfare of each, and therefore of all, that each is but a part of the one great whole, and each one stands shoulder to shoulder in the advance forward, can we hope for any true solution of the great social problems before us, for any permanent elevation of the standard in our national social life and welfare.

This same principle is the solution, and the only true solution, of the charities question, as indeed the whole world during the last few years or so, and during this time only, is beginning to realize. And the splendid and efficient work of the organized charities in all our large cities, as of the Elberfeld system in Germany, is attesting the truth of this. Almost numberless methods have been tried during the past, but all have most successfully failed; and many have greatly increased the wretched condition of matters, and of those it was designed to help. During this length of time only have these all-important questions been dealt with in a true, scientific, Christ-like, common-sense way. It has been found even here that nothing can take the place of the personal and friendly influences of a life built upon this principle of service.

The question of aiding the poor and needy has passed through three distinct phases of development in the world's history. In early times it was, "Each one for himself, and the devil take the hindmost." From the time of the Christ, and up to the last few years it has been, "Help others." Now it is, *"Help others to help themselves."* The wealthy society lady going down Fifth Avenue in New York, or Michigan Avenue in Chicago, or Charles Street in Baltimore, or Commonwealth Avenue in Boston, who flings a coin to one asking alms, is *not* the one who is doing a true act of charity; but, on the other hand, she may be doing the one she thus gives to and to society in general much more harm than good, as is many times the case. It is but a cheap, a very cheap way of buying ease for her sympathetic nature or her sense of duty. Never let the word "charity," which always includes the elements of interested service, true helpfulness, kindliness, and love, be debased by making it a synonym of mere giving, which may mean the flinging of a quarter in scorn or for show.

Recognizing the great truth that the best and only way to help another is to help him to help himself, and that the neglected classes need not so much alms as friends, the Organized Charities with their several branches in different parts of the city have their staffs of "friendly visitors," almost all voluntary, and from some of the best homes in the land. Then when a case of need comes to the notice of the society, one of these goes to the person or family as a *friend* to investigate, to find what circumstances have brought about these conditions, and, if found worthy of aid, present needs are supplied, an effort is made to secure work, and every effort is made to put them on their feet again, that self-respect may be regained, that hope may enter in; for there is scarcely anything that tends to make one lose his self-respect so quickly and so completely as to be compelled, or of his own accord, to ask for alms.

It is thus many times that a new life is entered upon, brightness and hope taking the place of darkness and despair. This is not the only call the friendly visitor makes; but he or she becomes a *true friend,* and makes regular visits as such. If by this method the one seeking charity is found to be an impostor, as is frequently the case, proper means of exposure are resorted to, that his or her progress in this course may be stopped. The organizations are thus doing a most valuable work, and one that will become more and more valuable as they are enabled to become better organized, the greatest need to-day being more with the true spirit to act as visiting friends.

It is this same great principle that has given birth to our college and university settlements and our neighborhood guilds which are so rapidly increasing, and which are destined to do a great and efficient work. Here a small colony of young women, many from our best homes, and the ablest graduates of our best colleges, and young men, many of them the ablest graduates of our best universities, take up their abode in the poorest parts of our large cities, to try by their personal influence and personal contact to raise the surrounding life to a higher plane. It is in these ways that the poor and the unfortunate are dealt with directly. Thus the classes mingle. Thus that sentimentalism which may do and which has done harm to these great problems, and by which the people it is designed to help may be hindered rather than helped, is done away with. Thus true aid and service are rendered, and the needy are really helped.

The one whose life is built upon this principle will not take up work of this kind as a "fad," or because it is "fashionable," but because it is right, true, Christ-like. The truly great and noble never fear thus to mingle with those poorer and less fortunate. It is only those who would like to be counted as great, but who are too small to be so recognized, and who, therefore, always thinking of self, put forth every effort to appear so. There is no surer test than this.

Very truly has it been said that "the greatest thing a man can do for God is to be kind to some of His other children." All children of the same Father, therefore all brothers, sisters. Man is next to God. Man is God incarnate. Humanity, therefore, cannot be very far from being next to godliness. Many people there are who are greatly concerned about serving God, as they term it. Their idea is to build great edifices with costly ornaments to Him. A great deal of their time is spent in singing songs and hallelujahs to Him, just as if *He* needed or wanted these for Himself, forgetting that He is far above being benefited by anything that we can say or do, forgetting that He doesn't want these, when for lack of them some of His children are starving for bread to eat or are dying for the bread of life.

Can you conceive of a God who is worthy of love and service, – and I speak most reverently, – who under such conditions would take a satisfaction in these things? I confess I am not able to. I can conceive of no way in which I can serve God only as I serve Him through my own life and through the lives of my fellow-men. This, certainly, is the only kind of service He needs or wants, or that is acceptable to Him. At one place we read, "He that says he loves God and loves not his fellow-men, is a liar; and the truth is not in him."

Even in religion I think we shall find that there is nothing greater or more important than this great principle of service, helpfulness, kindliness, and love. Is not Christianity, you ask, greater or more important? Why, bless you, is this any other than Christianity, is Christianity any other than this, – at least, if we take what the Master Teacher himself has said? For what, let us ask, is a Christian, – the real, not merely in name? A follower of Christ, one who does as he did, one who lives as he lived. And, again, who was Christ? He that healed the sick, clothed the naked, bound up the broken-hearted, sustained and encouraged the weak, the faltering, befriended and aided the poor, the needy, condemned the proud and the selfish, taught the people to live nobly, truly, grandly, to live in their higher, diviner selves, that the greatest among them should be their servant, and that his followers were those who lived as he lived. He spent all his time in the service of humanity. He gave his whole life in this way. He it was who went about doing good.

Is it your desire then, to be numbered among his followers, to bear that blessed name, the name "Christian"? Then sit at his feet, and learn of him, love him, do as he did, as he taught you to do, live as he lived, as he taught you to live, and you are a Christian, and not unless you do. True Christianity can be found in no other way.

Naught is the difference what one may call himself; for many call themselves by this name to whom Christ says it will one day be said, "I never knew you: depart from me, ye cursed." Naught is the difference what creeds one may subscribe to, what rites and ceremonies he may observe, how loud and how numerous his professions may be. All of these are but as a vain mockery, unless he *is* a Christian; and to be a Christian is, as we have found, to be a follower of Christ, to do as he did, to live as he lived. Then live the Christ life. Live so as to become at one with God, and dwell continually in this blessed at-one-ment. The trouble all along has been that so many have mistaken the mere person of the Christ, the mere physical Jesus, for his life, his spirit, his teachings, and have succeeded in getting no farther than this as yet, except in cases here and there.

Now and then a rare soul rises up, one with great power, great inspiration, and we wonder at his great power, his great inspiration, why it is. When we look deeply enough, however, we will find that one great fact will answer the question every time. It is living the life that brings the power. He is living the Christ life, not merely standing afar off and looking at it, admiring it, and saying, Yes, I believe, I believe, and ending it there. In other words, he has found the kingdom of heaven. He has found that it is not a place, but a condition; and the song continually arising from his heart is, There is joy, only joy.

The Master, you remember, said: "Seek ye not for the kingdom of heaven in tabernacles or in houses made with hands. Know ye not that the kingdom of heaven is within you?" He told in plain words where and how to find it. He then told how to find *all other* things, when he said, "Seek ye first the kingdom of heaven, and all these other things shall be added unto you." Now, do you wonder at his power, his inspiration, his abundance of all things? The trouble with so many is that they act as if they do not believe what the Master said. They do not take him at his word. They say one thing: they do another. Their acts give the lie to their words. Instead of taking him at his word, and living as if they had faith in him, they prefer to follow a series of old, outgrown, man-made theories, traditions, forms, ceremonies, and seem to be satisfied with the results. No, *to be a Christian is to live the Christ life,* the life of him who went about doing good, the life of him who came not to be ministered unto, but to minister.

We will find that this mighty principle of love and service is the greatest to live by in this life, and also one of the gates whereby all who would must enter the kingdom of heaven.

Again we have the Master's words. In his own and only description of the last judgment, after speaking of the Son of Man coming in all his glory and all the holy angels with him, of his sitting on the throne of his glory with all nations gathered before him, of the separation of this gathered multitude into two parts, the one on his right, the other on his left, he says: "Then shall the King say unto them on his right hand, Come, ye blessed of my Father, inherit the kingdom prepared for you from the foundation of the world. For I was an hungered, and ye gave me meat; I was thirsty, and ye gave me drink; I was a stranger, and ye took me in; naked, and ye clothed me; I was sick, and ye visited me; I was in prison, and ye came unto me. Then shall the righteous answer him, saying, Lord, when saw we *thee* an hungered, and fed *thee?* or thirsty, and gave *thee* drink? When saw we *thee* a stranger, and took *thee* in? or naked, and clothed *thee?* Or when saw we *thee* sick, or in prison, and came unto *thee?* And the King shall answer, and say unto them, Verily I say unto you, *Inasmuch as ye have done it unto one of the least of these my brethren, ye have done it unto me.*

"Then shall he say unto them on the left hand, Depart from me, ye cursed. For I was an hungered, and ye gave me no meat; I was thirsty, and ye gave me no drink; I was a stranger, and ye took me not in; sick, and in prison, and ye visited me not. Then shall they answer him, saying, Lord, when saw we *thee* an hungered, or athirst, or a stranger, or naked, or sick, or in prison, and did not minister unto thee? Then shall he answer them, saying, Verily I say unto you, *Inasmuch as ye did it not to one of the least of these, ye did it not to me.*"

After spending the greater portion of his life in many distant climes in a fruitless endeavor to find the Cup of the Holy Grail,[3] thinking that thereby he was doing the greatest service he could for God, Sir Launfal at last returns an old man, gray-haired and bent. He finds that his castle is occupied by others, and that he himself is an outcast. His cloak is torn; and instead of the charger in gilded trappings he was mounted upon when as a young man, he started out with great hopes and ambitions, he is afoot and leaning on a staff. While sitting there and meditating, he is met by the same poor and needy leper he passed the morning he started, the one who in his need asked for aid, and to whom he had flung a coin in scorn, as he hurried on in his eager desire to be in the

---

3   "According to the mythology of the Romancers, the Sangreal, or Holy Grail, was the cup out of which Jesus partook of the Last Supper with his disciples. It was brought into England by Joseph of Arimathea, and remained there, an object of pilgrimage and adoration, for many years in the keeping of his lineal descendants. It was incumbent upon those who had charge of it to be chaste in thought, word, and deed; but, one of the keepers having broken this condition, the Holy Grail disappeared. From that time it was a favorite enterprise of the Knights of Sir Arthur's court to go in search of it."

James Russell Lowell.

Master's service. But matters are changed now, and he is a wiser man. Again the poor leper says: –

"'For Christ's sweet sake, I beg an alms'; –
The happy camels may reach the spring,
But Sir Launfal sees only the grewsome thing,
The leper, lank as the rain-blanched bone,
That cowers beside him, a thing as lone
And white as the ice-isles of Northern seas
In the desolate horror of his disease.

"And Sir Launfal said: 'I behold in thee
An image of Him who died on the tree;
Thou also hast had thy crown of thorns, –
Thou also hast had the world's buffets and scorns, –
And to thy life were not denied
The wounds in the hands and feet and side:
Mild Mary's Son, acknowledge me;
Behold, through him, I give to thee!'

"Then the soul of the leper stood up in his eyes
And looked at Sir Launfal, and straightway be
Remembered in what a haughtier guise
He had flung an alms to leprosie,
When he girt his young life up in gilded mail
And set forth in search of the Holy Grail.
The heart within him was ashes and dust;
He parted in twain his single crust,
He broke the ice on the streamlet's brink,
And gave the leper to eat and drink,
'Twas a mouldy crust of coarse brown bread,
'Twas water out of a wooden bowl, –
Yet with fine wheaten bread was the leper fed,
And 'twas red wine he drank with his thirsty soul.

"As Sir Launfal mused with a downcast face,
A light shone round about the place;
The leper no longer crouched at his side,
But stood before him glorified,
Shining and tall and fair and straight
As the pillar that stood by the Beautiful Gate, –

Himself the Gate whereby men can
Enter the temple of God in Man.

"And the voice that was calmer than silence said,
'Lo, it is I, be not afraid!
In many climes, without avail,
Thou hast spent thy life for the Holy Grail;
Behold, it is here, – this cup which thou
Didst fill at the streamlet for me but now;
This crust is my body broken for thee,
This water His blood that died on the tree;
The Holy Supper is kept, indeed,
In whatso we share with another's need;
Not what we give, but what we share, –
For the gift without the giver is bare;
Who gives himself with his alms feeds three, –
Himself, his hungering neighbor, and me.'"

The fear is sometimes entertained, and the question is sometimes asked, May not adherence to this principle of helpfulness
and service become mere sentimentalism? or still more, may it
not be the means of lessening another's sense of self-dependence,
and thus may it not at times do more harm than good? In reply
let it be said: If the love which impels it be a selfish love, or a weak
sentimental ism, or an effort at show, or devoid of good common
sense, yes, many times. But if it be a strong, genuine, unselfish
love, then no, never. For, if my love for my fellow-man be the true
love, I can never do anything that will be to his or any one's else
detriment, – nothing that will not redound to his highest ultimate
welfare. Should he, for example come and ask of me a particular
favor, and were it clear to me that granting it would not be for
his highest good ultimately, then love at once resolves itself into
duty, and compels me to forbear. A true, genuine, unselfish love
for one's fellow-man will never prompt, and much less permit,
anything that will not result in his highest ultimate good. Adherence, therefore, to this great principle in its truest sense, instead
of being a weak sentimentalism, is, we shall find, of all practical
things the *most intensely practical.*

And a word here in regard to the test of true love and service, in distinction from its semblance for show or for vain glory.
The test of the true is this: that it goes about and does its good

work, it never says anything about it, but lets others do the saying. It not only says nothing about it, but more, it has no desire to have it known; and, the truer it is, the greater the desire to have it unknown save to God and its own true self. In other words, it is not sicklied o'er with a semi-insane desire for notoriety or vainglory, and hence never weakens itself nor harasses any one else by lengthy recitals of its good deeds. It is not the *professional* good-doing. It is simply living its natural life, open-minded, open-hearted, doing each day what its hands find to do, and in this finding its own true life and joy. And in this way it unintentionally but irresistibly draws to itself a praise the rarest and divinest I know of, – the praise I heard given but a day or two ago to one who is living simply his own natural life without any conscious effort at anything else, the praise contained in the words: And, oh, it is beautiful, the great amount of good he does and of which the world never hears.

PART V

THE INCOMING

O dull, gray grub, unsightly and noisome, unable to roam,
Days pass, God's at work, the slow chemistry's going on,
Behold! Behold!
O brilliant, buoyant life, full winged, all the heaven's thy home!
O poor, mean man, stumbling and falling, e'en shamed by a clod.
Years pass, God's at work, spiritual awakening has come,
Behold! Behold!
O regal, royal soul, then image, now the likeness of God.

THE Master Teacher, he who appeals most strongly and comes nearest to us of this western civilization, has told us that the whole and the highest duty of man is comprised in two great, two simple precepts – love to God and love to the fellow-man. The latter we have already fully considered. We have found that in its real and true meaning it is not a mere indefinite or sentimental abstraction, but that it is a vital, living force; and in its manifestation it is life, it is action, it is service. Let us now for a moment to the other, – love to God, which in great measure however let it be said, has been considered in dealing with love to the fellow-man. Let us see, however, what it in its true and full nature reveals.

The question naturally arising at the outset is, Who, what is God? I think no truer, sublimer definition has ever been given in the world's history, in any language, in any clime, than that given by the Master himself when standing by the side of Jacob's well, to the Samaritan woman he said, God is Spirit; and they that worship Him must worship Him in spirit and in truth. God is Spirit, the Infinite Spirit, the Infinite Life back of all these physical manifestations we see in this changing world about us, and of which all, including we ourselves, is the body or outer form; the one Infinite Spirit which fills all the universe with Himself, so that all is He, since He is all. All is He in the sense of being a part of Him; for, if He is all, there can be nothing that is outside of, that is not a part of Him, so that each one is a part of this Eternal God who is not separate from us, and, if not separate from us, then not afar off, for in Him we live and move and have our being, *He is the life of our life,* our very life itself. The life of God is in us, we are in the life of God; but that life transcends us so that it includes all else, – every person, every animal, every grass-blade, every flower, every particle of earth, every particle of everything, animate and inanimate. So that God is *All;* and, if all, then each individual, you and I, must be a vital part of that all, since there can be nothing separate from it; and, if a part, then the same in nature, in characteristics, – the same as a tumbler of water taken from the ocean is, in nature, in qualities, in characteristics, identical with that ocean, its source. God, then, is the Infinite Spirit of which each one is a part in the form of an individualized spirit. God is Spirit, creating, manifesting, ruling through the agency of great spiritual laws and forces that surround us on every side, that run through all the universe, and that unite all; for in one sense, there is nothing in all this great universe but law. And, oh, the stupendous grandeur of it all! These same great spiritual laws and forces operate within us. They are the laws of our being. By them every act of each individual life is governed.

Now one of the great facts borne ever more and more into the inner consciousness of man is that sublime and transcendent fact that we have just noticed, – that man is one with, that he is part of, the Infinite God, this Infinite Spirit that is the life of all, this Infinite Whole; that he is not a mere physical, material being, – for the physical is but the material which the real inner self, the real life or spirit uses to manifest through, – but that he *is* this spirit, this spirit, using, living in this physical, material house or body to get the contact, the experience with the material world around him while in this form of life, but spirit nevertheless, and spirit now as much as he ever will or ever can be, except so far of course, as he recognizes more and more his true, his higher self, and so consciously evolves, step by step, into the higher and ever higher realization of the real nature, the real self, the God-self. As

I heard it said by one of the world's great thinkers and writers but a few days ago: Men talk of having a soul. I have no soul. I am a soul: I have a body. We are told moreover in the word, that man is created in the image of God. God is Spirit. What then must man be, if that which tells us is true?

Now one of the great errors all along in the past has been that we have mistaken the mere body, the mere house in which we live while in this form of life for a period, – that which comes from the earth and which, in a greater or less time, returns to the earth, – this we have mistaken for the real self. Either we have lost sight of or we have failed to recognize the true identity. The result is that we are at life from the wrong side, from the side of the external, while all true life is from within out.

We have taken our lives out of a conscious harmony with the higher laws of our being, with the result that we are going against the great current of the Divine Order of things. Is it any wonder, then, that we find the strugglings, the inharmonies, the sufferings, the fears, the forebodings, the fallings by the wayside, the "strange, inscrutable dispensations of Providence" that we behold on every side? The moment we bring our lives into harmony with the higher laws of our being, and, as a result, into harmony with the current of the Divine Order of things, we shall find that all these will have taken wings; for the cause will have been removed. And as we look down the long vista of such a life, we shall find that each thing fits into all others with a wonderful, a sublime, a perfect, a divine harmony.

This, it will seem to some, – and to many, no doubt, – is claiming a great deal. No more, however, than the Master Teacher warranted us in claiming when he said, and repeated it so often, Seek ye first the kingdom of heaven, and all these other things shall be added unto you; and he left us not in the dark as to exactly what he meant by the kingdom of heaven, for again he said: Say not, Lo here, nor lo there. Know ye not that the kingdom of heaven is within you? *Within you.* The interior spiritual kingdom, the kingdom of the higher self, which is the kingdom of God; the kingdom of harmony, – harmony with the higher laws of your being.

The Master said what he said not for the sake merely of using a phrase of rhetoric, nor even to hear himself talk; for this he never did. But that great incarnation of spiritual insight and power knew of the great spiritual laws and forces under which we live, and also that supreme fact of the universe, that *man is a spiritual being, born to have dominion,* and that, by recognizing the true self and by bringing it into complete and perfect harmony with the higher spiritual laws and forces under which he lives, he can touch these laws and forces so that they will respond at every call and bring him whatsoever he wills, – one of the most stupendous scientific facts of the universe. When he has found and entered into the kingdom, then applies to him the truth of the great precept, Take ye no thought for the morrow; for the things of the morrow will take care of themselves.

Yes, we are at life from the wrong side. We have been giving all time and attention to the mere physical, the material, the external, the mere outward means of expression and the things that pertain thereto, thus missing the real life; and this we have called living, and seem, indeed, to be satisfied with the results. No wonder the cry has gone out again and again from many a human soul, Is life worth the living? But from one who has once commenced to *live,* this cry never has, nor can it ever come; for, *when the kingdom is once found, life then ceases to be a plodding, and becomes an exultation, an ecstasy, a joy.* Yes, you will find that all the evil, all the error, all the disease, all the suffering, all the fears, all the forebodings of life, are on the side of the physical, the material, the transient; while all the peace, all the joy, all the happiness, all the growth, all the life, all the rich, exulting, abounding life, is on the side of the spiritual, the ever-increasing, the eternal, – that that never changes, that has no end. Instead of crying out against the destiny of fate, let us cry out against the destiny of self, or rather against the destiny of the mistaken self; for everything that comes to us comes through causes which we ourselves or those before us have set into operation. Nothing comes by chance, for *in all the wide universe there is absolutely no such thing as chance.* We bring whatever comes. Are we not satisfied with the effects, the results? The thing then to do, is to change the causes; for we have everything in our own hands the moment we awake to a recognition of the true self.

We make our own heaven or our own hell, and the only heaven or hell that will ever be ours is that of our own making. The order of the universe is one thing: we take our lives out of harmony with and so pervert the laws under which we live, and make it another. The order is the all good. We pervert the laws, and what we call evil is the result, – simply the result of the violation of law; and we then wonder that a just and loving God could permit such and such things. We wonder at what we term the "strange, inscrutable dispensations of Providence," when all is of our own making. We can be our own best friends or we can be our own worst enemies; and the only real enemy one can ever have is the self, the very self.

It is a well-known fact in the scientific world that the great work in the process of evolution is the gradual advancing from the lower to the higher, from the coarser to the finer, or, in other words, from the coarser material to the finer spiritual; and this higher spiritualization of life is the great work before us all. All pass ultimately over the same road in general, some more rapidly, some more slowly. The ultimate destiny of all is the higher life, the finding of the higher self; and to this we are either led or we are pushed, – led, by recognizing and coming into harmony with the higher laws of our being, or pushed, through their violation, and hence through experience, through suffering, and at times through bitter suffering, until through this very agency we learn the laws and come into harmony with them, so that we thus see the economy, the blessedness of even error, shame, and suffering itself, in that, if we are not wise enough to go voluntarily and of our own accord, it all the more quickly brings us to our true, our higher selves.

Moreover, whatever is evolved must as surely first be involved. We cannot conceive even of an evolution without first an involution; and, if this is true, we cannot conclude otherwise than that all that will ever be brought forth through the process of evolution is already within, all the God possibilities of the human soul are now, at this very moment, latent within. This being true, the process of evolution need not, as is many times supposed, take aeons or even ages for its accomplishment; for the process is wonderfully accelerated when we have grasped and when we have commenced to actualize the reality of that mighty precept, Know thyself.

It is possible, through an intelligent understanding of the laws of the higher life, to advance in the spiritual awakening and unfoldment even in a single year more than one otherwise would through a whole lifetime, or more in a single day or even hour than in an entire year or series of years otherwise.

This higher spiritualization of life is certainly what the Master had in mind when he said, It is as hard for a rich man to enter into the kingdom of heaven as it is for a camel to pass through the eye of a needle. For, if a man give all his days and his nights merely to the accumulation of outer material possessions, what time has he for the growing, the unfolding, of the interior, the spiritual, what time for finding that wonderful kingdom, the kingdom of heaven, the Christ within?

This certainly is also the significance of the temptation in the wilderness. The temptations were all, you will recall, in connection with the material, the physical, and the things that pertain thereto. Do so and so, said the physical: follow after me, and I will give you bread in abundance, I will give you great fame and notoriety, I will give you vast material possessions. All, you see, a calling away from the real, the interior, the spiritual, the eternal. Dominion over all the kingdoms of the *world* was promised. But what, what is dominion overall the world, with heaven left out?

All, however, was triumphed over. The physical was put into subjection by the spiritual, the victory was gained once for all and forever; and he became the supreme and royal Master, and by this complete and glorious mastery of self he gained the mastery over all else besides, even to material things and conditions.

And by this higher spiritual chemicalization of life thus set into operation the very thought forces of his mind became charged with a living, mighty, and omnipotent power, so as to effect a mastery over all exterior conditions: hence the numerous things called miracles by those who witnessed and who had not entered into a knowledge of the higher laws that can triumph over and master the lower, but which are just as real and as natural on their plane as the lower, and even more real and more natural, because higher and therefore more enduring. But this complete mastery over self during this period of temptation was just the beginning of the path that led from glory unto glory, the path that for you and for me will lead from glory unto glory the same as for him.

It was this new divine and spiritual chemistry of life thus set into operation that transformed the man Jesus, that royal-hearted elder brother, into the Christ Jesus, and forever blessed be his name; for he thus became our Saviour, – he became our Saviour by virtue of pointing out to us the way. This overcoming by the calling of the higher spiritual forces into operation is certainly what he meant when he said, I have overcome the world, and what he would have us understand when he says, Overcome the world, even as I have overcome it.

And in the same sense we are all the saviors one of another, or may become so. A sudden emergency arises, and I stand faltering and weak with fear. My friend beside me is strong and fearless. He sees the emergency. He summons up all the latent powers within him, and springs forth to meet it. This sublime example arouses me, calls my latent powers into activity, when but for him I might not have known them there. I follow his example. I now know my powers, and know them forever after. Thus, in this, my friend has become my savior.

I am weak in some point of character, – vacillating, yielding, stumbling, falling, continually eating the bitter fruit of it all. My friend is strong, he has gained thorough self-mastery. The majesty and beauty of power are upon his brow. I see his example, I love his life, I am influenced by his power. My soul longs and cries out for the same. A supreme effort of will – that imperial master that will take one anywhere when rightly directed – arises within me, it is born at last, and it calls all the soul's latent powers into activity; and instead of stumbling I stand firm, instead of giving over in weakness I stand firm and master, I enter into the joys of full self-mastery, and through this into the mastery of all things besides. And thus my friend has again become my savior.

With the new power I have acquired through the example and influence of my savior-friend, I, in turn, stand before a friend who is struggling, who is stumbling and in despair. He sees, he feels, the power of my strength. He longs for, his soul cries out for the same. *His* interior forces are called into activity, he now knows his powers; and instead of the slave, he becomes the master, and thus I, in turn, have become his savior. Oh, the wonderful sense of sublimity, the mighty feelings of responsibility, the deep sense of power and peace the recognition of this fact should bring to each and all.

God works through the instrumentality of human agency. Then forever away with that old, shrivelling, weakening, dying, and devilish idea that we are poor worms of the dust! We may or we may not be: it all depends upon the self. The moment we believe we are we become such; and as long as we hold to the belief we will be held to this identity, and will act and live as such. The moment, however, we recognize our divinity, our higher, our God-selves, and the fact that we are the saviors of our fellow-men, we become saviors, and stand and move in the midst of a majesty and beauty and power that of itself proclaims us as such.

ℰℐ

There is a prevalent idea to the effect that overcoming in this sense necessarily implies more or less of a giving up, – that it means something possibly on the order of asceticism. On the contrary, the highest, truest, keenest pleasures the human soul can know, it finds only after the higher is entered upon and has commenced its work of mastery; and, instead of there being a giving up of any kind, there is a great law which says that the lower always and of its own accord falls away before the higher. And the time soon comes when, as one stands and looks back, he wonders that this or that that he at one time called pleasure ever satisfied him; for what then satisfied him, compared to what now is his hourly peace, satisfaction, and joy, was but as poor brass compared to the finest, purest, and rarest of gold.

From what has been said let it not be inferred that the body, the physical, material life is to be despised or looked down upon. This, rather let it be said, is one of the crying errors of the times, and prolific of a *vast* amount of error, suffering, and shame. On the contrary, it should be thought all the more highly of: it should be loved and developed to its highest perfections, beauties, and powers. God gave us the body not in vain. It is just as holy and beautiful as the spirit itself. It is merely the outward material manifestation of the individualized spirit; and we by our hourly thoughts and emotions are building it, are determining its conditions, its structure, and appearance. And, if there are any conditions we are not satisfied with, we by an understanding of the laws, have it in our power to make it over and change these conditions. Flamarion, the eminent French scientist, member of the Royal Academy of Science, and recognized as one of the most eminent scientists living, tells us that the entire human structure can be made over within a period of less than one year, some eleven months being the length of time required for the more compact and more set portions to respond; while some portions respond much more readily within a period of from two to three months, and some even within a month.

Every part, every organ, every function of the body is just as clean, just as beautiful, just as sweet, and just as holy as every other part; and it is only by virtue of man's perverted ways of looking at some that they become otherwise, and the moment they so become, abuses, ill uses, suffering, and shame creep in.

Not repression, but elevation. Would that this could be repeated a thousand times over! Not repression, but elevation. Every part, every organ, every function of the body is given for *use,* but not for misuse or abuse; and the moment the latter takes place in connection with any function it loses its higher powers of use, and there goes with this the higher powers of true enjoyment. It is thus that we get that large class known as abnormals, resorting to the methods they resort to for enjoyment, but which, in its true sense, they always fail in finding, because law will admit of no violations; and, if violated, it takes away the very powers of enjoyment, it takes away the very things that through its violation they thought they had secured, or it turns them into ashes in their very hands. God, nature, law, the higher self, is not mocked.

Not repression, but elevation, – repression only in the sense of mastery; but this means – nay, this is – elevation. In other words, we should be the master, and not the body. We should dictate to the body, and should never, even for an instant, allow it to dictate to us.

Oh, the thousands, the hundreds of thousands of men and women who are everywhere being driven hither and thither, led into this and into that which their own better selves would not enter into, simply because they have allowed the body to assume the mastery; while they have taken the place of the weakling, the slave, and all on account of their own weakness, – weakness through ignorance, ignorance of the tremendous forces and powers within, the forces and powers of the mind and spirit.

It would be a right royal plan for those who are thus enslaved by the body, – and we all are more or less, each in his own particular way, and not one is absolutely free, – it would be a good plan to hold immediately, at this very hour, a conversation with the body somewhat after this fashion: Body, we have for some time been dwelling together. Life for neither has been in the highest degree satisfactory. The cause is now apparent to me. The mastery I have voluntarily handed over to you. You have not assumed it of your own accord; but I have given it over to you little by little, and just in the degree that you have appropriated it. Neither one is to blame. It has been by virtue of ignorance. But henceforth we will reverse positions. You shall become the servant, and I the master. From this time forth you shall no longer dictate to me, but I will dictate to you.

I, one with Infinite intelligence, wisdom, and power, longing for a fuller and ever fuller realization of this oneness, will assume control, and will call upon you to help in the fuller and ever fuller external manifestation of this realization. We will thus regain the ground both of us have lost. We will thus be truly married instead of farcically so. And thus we will help each the other to a realization of the highest, most satisfying and most enduring pleasures and joys, possibilities and powers, loves and realizations, that human life can know; and so, hand in hand, we will help each the other to the higher and ever-increasing life instead of degrading each the other to the lower and ever-decreasing. I will become the imperial master, and you the royal companion; and thus we will go forth to an ever larger life of love and service, and so of true enjoyment.

This conversation, if entered into in the spirit, accompanied by an earnest, sincere desire for its fulfilment, re-enforced by the thought forces, and continually attended by that absolute magnet of power, firm expectation, will, if all are firmly and persistently held to, bring the full realization of one's fondest desires with a certainty as absolute as that effect follows cause. The higher self will invariably master when it truly and firmly asserts itself. Much the same attitude can be assumed in connection with the body in disease or in suffering with the same results. Forces can be set into operation which will literally change and make over the diseased, the abnormal portions, and in time transform them into the healthy, the strong, the normal, – this when we once understand and vitally grasp the laws of these mighty forces, and are brought to the full recognition of the absolute control of mind, of spirit, over matter, and all, again let it be said, in accordance with natural spiritual law.

No, a knowledge of the spiritual realities of life prohibits asceticism, repression, the same as it prohibits license and perverted use. To err on the one side is just as contrary to the ideal life as to err on the other. All things are for a purpose, all should be used and enjoyed; but all should be rightly used, that they may be fully enjoyed.

It is the threefold life and development that is wanted, – physical, mental, spiritual. This gives the rounded life, and he or she who fails in any one comes short of the perfect whole. The physical has its uses just the same and is just as important as the others. The great secret of the highly successful life is, however, to infuse the mental and the physical with the spiritual; in other words, to spiritualize all, and so raise all to the highest possibilities and powers.

It is the all-round, fully developed we want, – not the ethereal, pale-blooded man and woman, but the man and woman of flesh and blood, for action and service here and now, – the man and woman strong and powerful, with all the faculties and functions fully unfolded and used, all in a royal and bounding condition, but all rightly subordinated. The man and the woman of this kind, with the imperial hand of mastery upon all, – standing, moving thus like a king, nay, like a very God, – such is the man and such is the woman of power. Such is the ideal life: anything else is one-sided, and falls short of it.

಼

The most powerful agent in character-building is this awakening to the true self, to the fact that man is a spiritual being, – nay, more, that I, this very eternal I, am a spiritual being, right here and now, at this very moment, with the God-powers which can be quickly called forth. With this awakening, life in all its manifold relations becomes wonderfully simplified. And as to the powers, the full realization of the fact that man is a spiritual being and a living as such brings, they are absolutely without limit, increasing in direct proportion as the higher self, the God-self, assumes the mastery, and so as this higher spiritualization of life goes on.

With this awakening and realization one is brought at once *en rapport* with the universe. He feels the power and the thrill of the life universal. He goes out from his own little garden spot, and mingles with the great universe; and the little perplexities, trials, and difficulties of life that to-day so vex and annoy him, fall away of their own accord by reason of their very insignificance. The intuitions become keener and ever more keen and unerring in their guidance. There comes more and more the power of reading men, so that no harm can come from this source. There comes more and more the power of seeing into the future, so that more and more true becomes the old adage, – that coming events cast their shadows before. Health in time takes the place of disease; for all disease and its consequent suffering is merely the result of the violation of law, either consciously or unconsciously, either intentionally or unintentionally. There comes also a spiritual power which, as it is sent out, is adequate for the healing of others the same as in the days of old. The body becomes less gross and heavy, finer in its texture and form, so that it serves far better and responds far more readily to the higher impulses of the soul. Matter itself in time responds to the action of these higher forces; and many things that we are accustomed by reason of our limited vision to call miraculous or supernatural become the normal, the natural, the every-day.

For what, let us ask, is a miracle? Nothing more nor less than this: a highly illumined soul, one who has brought his life into thorough harmony with the higher spiritual laws and forces of his being, and therefore with those of the universe, thus making it possible for the highest things to come to him, has brought to him a law a little higher than the ordinary mind knows of as yet. This he touches, he operates. It responds. The people see the result, and cry out, Miracle! miracle! when it is just as natural, just as fully in accordance with the law on this higher plane, as is the common, the every-day on the ordinary. And let it be remembered that the miraculous, the supernatural of to-day becomes, as in the process of evolution we leave the lower for the higher, the commonplace, the natural, the every-day of to-morrow; and, truly, miracles are being performed in the world to-day just as much as they ever have been.

And why should we not to-day have the powers of the foremost in the days of old? The great universe in which we live is just the same, the great laws under which we live are identically the same, God the same and working in His world now just as then. The only difference we shall find is in ourselves, in that we have taken our lives out of harmony with the higher laws of our being, and consequently have lost the higher powers through not using them. Mighty men we are told they were, mighty men who walked with God, – and in the last clause lies the secret of the first, – men who lived in the spirit, men who followed after the real life instead of giving all time and attention to the mere external, men who lived in the higher stories of their being, and not continually in the basements.

With here and there an exception we reverse the process. We live in the valleys, so to speak, often disease-infected valleys, when we might mount up to the mountain-tops, and there dwell continually in the warm and mellow sunlight of God's, or if you please, of nature's great, unchangeable laws, and find ourselves rising ever higher and higher, and revelations coming new every day.

The Master never claimed for himself anything that he did not claim for all mankind; but, quite to the contrary, he said and continually repeated, Not only shall ye do these things, but greater than these shall ye do; for I have pointed out to you the way, – meaning, though strange as it evidently seems to many, *exactly* what he said.

Of the vital power of thought and the interior forces in moulding conditions, and more, of the supremacy of thought over all conditions, the world has scarcely the faintest grasp, not to say even idea, as yet. The fact that thoughts are forces, and that through them *we have creative power,* is one of the most vital facts of the universe, the most vital fact of man's being. And through this instrumentality we have in our grasp and as our rightful heritage, the power of making life and all its manifold conditions exactly what we will.

Through our thought-forces we have creative power, not in a figurative sense, but in reality. Everything in the material universe about us had its origin first in spirit, in thought, and from this it took its form. The very world in which we live, with all its manifold wonders and sublime manifestations, is the result of the energies of the divine intelligence or mind, – God, or whatever term it comes convenient for each one to use. And God said, Let there be, and there was, – the material world, at least the material manifestation of it, literally spoken into existence, the spoken word, however, but the outward manifestation of the interior forces of the Supreme Intelligence.

Every castle the world has ever seen was first an ideal in the architect's mind. Every statue was first an ideal in the sculptor's mind. Every piece of mechanism the world has ever known was first formed in the mind of the inventor. Here it was given birth to. These same mind-forces then dictated to and sent the energy into the hand that drew the model, and then again dictated to and sent the energy into the hands whereby the first instrument was clothed in the material form of metal or of wood. The lower negative always gives way to the higher when made positive. Mind is positive: matter is negative.

Each individual life is a part of, and hence is one with, the Infinite Life; and the highest intelligence and power belongs to each in just the degree that he recognizes his oneness and lays claim to and uses it. The power of the word is not merely an idle phrase or form of expression. It is a real mental, spiritual, scientific fact, and can become vital and powerful in your hands and in mine in just the degree that we understand the omnipotence of the thought forces and raise all to the higher planes.

The blind, the lame, the diseased, stood before the Christ, who said, Receive thy sight, rise up and walk, or, be thou healed; and o! *it was so.* The spoken word, however, was but the outward expression and manifestation of his interior thought-forces, the power and potency of which he so thoroughly knew. But the laws governing them are the same to-day as they were then, and it lies in our power to use them the same as it lay in his.

Each individual life, after it has reached a certain age or degree of intelligence, lives in the midst of the surroundings or environments of its own creation; and this by reason of that wonderful power, *the drawing power of mind,* which is continually operating in every life, whether it is conscious of it or not.

We are all living, so to speak, in a vast ocean of thought. The very atmosphere about us is charged with the thought-forces that are being continually sent out. When the thought-forces leave the brain, they go out upon the atmosphere, the subtle conducting ether, much the same as sound-waves go out. It is by virtue of this law that thought transference is possible, and has become an established scientific fact, by virtue of which a person can so direct his thought-forces that a person at a distance, and in a receptive attitude, can get the thought much the same as sound, for example, is conducted through the agency of a connecting medium.

Even though the thoughts as they leave a particular person, are not consciously directed, they go out; and all may be influenced by them in a greater or less degree, each one in proportion as he or she is more or less sensitively organized, or in proportion as he or she is negative, and so open to forces and influences from without. The law operating here is one with that great law of the universe, – that like attracts like, so that one continually attracts to himself forces and influences most akin to those of his own life.

And his own life is determined by the thoughts and emotions he habitually entertains, for each is building his world from within. As within, so without; cause, effect.

A stalk of wheat and a stock of corn are growing side by side, within an inch of each other. The soil is the same for both; but the wheat converts the food it takes from the soil into wheat, the likeness of itself, while the corn converts the food it takes from the same soil into corn, the likeness of itself. What that which each has taken from the soil is converted into is determined by the soul, the interior life, the interior forces of each. This same grain taken as food by two persons will be converted into the body of a criminal in the one case, and into the body of a saint in the other, each after its kind; and its kind is determined by the inner life of each. And what again determines the inner life of each? The thoughts and emotions that are habitually entertained and that inevitably, sooner or later, manifest themselves in outer material form. Thought is the great builder in human life: it is the determining factor. Continually think thoughts that are good, and your life will show forth in goodness, and your body in health and beauty. Continually think evil thoughts, and your life will show forth in evil, and your body in weakness and repulsiveness. Think thoughts of love, and you will love and will be loved. Think thoughts of hatred, and you will hate and will be hated. Each follows its kind.

It is by virtue of this law that each person creates his own "atmosphere"; and this atmosphere is determined by the character of the thoughts he habitually entertains. It is, in fact, simply his thought atmosphere – the atmosphere which other people detect and are influenced by.

In this way each person creates the atmosphere of his own room; a family, the atmosphere of the house in which they live, so that the moment you enter the door you feel influences kindred to the thoughts and hence to the lives of those who dwell there. You get a feeling of peace and harmony or a feeling of disquietude and inharmony. You get a welcome, want-to-stay feeling or a cold, want-to-get-away feeling, according to their thought attitude toward you, even though but few words be spoken. So the characteristic mental states of a congregation of people who assemble there determine the atmosphere of any given assembly-place, church, or cathedral. Its inhabitants so make, so determine the atmosphere of a particular village or city. The sympathetic thoughts sent out by a vast amphitheatre of people, as they cheer a contestant, carry him to goals he never could reach by his own efforts alone. The same is true in regard to an orator and his audience.

Napoleon's army is in the East. The plague is beginning to make inroads into its ranks. Long lines of men are lying on cots and on the ground in an open space adjoining the army. Fear has taken a vital hold of all, and the men are continually being stricken. Look yonder, contrary to the earnest entreaties of his officers, who tell him that such exposure will mean sure death, Napoleon with a calm and dauntless look upon his face, with a firm and defiant step, is coming through these plague-stricken ranks. He is going up to, talking with, touching the men; and, as they see him, there goes up a mighty shout, – The Emperor! the Emperor! and from that hour the plague in its inroads is stopped. A marvellous example of the power of a man who, by his own dauntless courage, absolute fearlessness, and power of mind, could send out such forces that they in turn awakened kindred forces in the minds of thousands of others, which in turn dominate their very bodies, so that the plague, and even death itself, is driven from the field. One of the grandest examples of a man of the most mighty and tremendous mind and will power, and at the same time an example of one of the grandest failures, taking life in its totality, the world has ever seen.

Again, as has been said, the great law operating in connection with the thought-forces is one with that great law of the universe, – that like attracts like. We can, by virtue of our ignorance of the powers of the mind forces and the prevailing mental states, – we can take the passive, the negative, fearing, drifting attitude, and thus continually attract to us like influences and conditions from both the seen and the unseen side of life. Or, by a knowledge of the power and potency of these forces, we can take the positive, the active attitude, that of mastery, and so attract the higher and more valuable influences, exactly as we will to.

We are all much more influenced by the thought-forces and mental states of those around us and of the world at large than we have even the slightest conception of. If not self-hypnotized into certain beliefs and practices, we are, so to speak, semi-hypnotized through the influence of the thoughts of others, even though unconsciously both on their part and on ours. We are so influenced and enslaved in just the degree that we fail to recognize the power and omnipotence of our own forces, and so become slaves to custom, conventionality, the opinions of others, and so in like proportion lose our own individuality and powers. He who in his own mind takes the attitude of the slave, by the power of his own thoughts and the forces he thus attracts to him, becomes the slave. He who in his own mind takes the attitude of the master, by the same power of his own thoughts and the forces he thus attracts to him, becomes the master. Each is building his world from within, and, if outside forces play, it is because he allows them to play; and he has it in his own power to determine whether these shall be positive, uplifting, ennobling, strengthening, success-giving, or negative, degrading, weakening, failure-bringing.

Nothing is more subtle than thought, nothing more powerful, nothing more irresistible in its operations, when rightly applied and held to with a faith and fidelity that is unswerving, – a faith and fidelity that never knows the neutralizing effects of doubt and fear. If one have aspirations and a sincere desire for a higher and better condition, so far as advantages, facilities, associates, or any surroundings or environments are concerned, and if he continually send out his highest thought-forces for the realization of these desires, and continually water these forces with firm expectation as to their fulfilment, he will sooner or later find himself in the realization of these desires, and all in accordance with natural laws and forces.

Fear brings its own fulfilment the same as hope. The same law operates, and if, as our good and valued friend, Job, said when the darkest days were setting in upon him, – that which I feared has come upon me, – was true, how much more surely could he have brought about the opposite conditions, those he would have desired, had he have had even the slightest realization of his own powers, and had he acted the part of the master instead of that of the servant, had he have dictated terms instead of being dictated to, and thus suffering the consequences.

If one finds himself in any particular condition, in the midst of any surroundings or environments that are not desirable, that have nothing – at least for any length of time – that is of value to him, for his highest life and unfoldment, he has the remedy entirely within his own grasp the moment he realizes the power and supremacy of the forces of the mind and spirit; and, unless he intelligently use these forces, he drifts. Unless through them he becomes master and dictates, he becomes the slave and is dictated to, and so is driven hither and thither.

Earnest, sincere desire, sincere aspiration for higher and better conditions or means to realize them, the thought-forces actively sent out for their realization, these continually watered by firm expectation without allowing the contrary, neutralizing force of fear ever to enter in, – this, accompanied by rightly directed work and activity, will bring about the fullest realization of one's highest desires and aspirations with a certainty as absolute as that effect follows cause. Each and every one of us can thus make for himself ever higher and higher conditions, can attract ever and ever higher influences, can realize an ever higher and higher ideal in life. These are the forces that are within us, simply waiting to be recognized and used, – the forces that we should infuse into and mould every-day life with. The moment we vitally recognize them, they become our servants and wait upon our bidding.

Are you, for example, a young man or a young woman desiring a college, a university education, or have you certain literary or artistic instincts your soul longs the more fully to realize and actualize, and seems there no way open for you to realize the fulfilment of your desires? But the power is in your hands the moment you recognize it there. Begin at once to set the right forces into operation. Put forth your ideal, which will begin to clothe itself in material form, send out your thought-forces for its realization, continually hold and add to them, always strongly but always calmly, never allow the element of fear, which will keep the realization just so much farther away, to enter in; but, on the contrary, continually water with firm expectation all the forces thus set into operation. Do not then sit and idly fold the hands, expecting to see all things drop into the lap, – God feeds the sparrow, but he does not throw the food into its nest, – but take hold of the first thing that offers itself for you to do, – work in the fields, at the desk, saw wood, wash dishes, tend behind the counter, or whatever it may be, – be faithful to the thing in hand, always expecting something better, and know that this in hand is the thing that will open to you the next higher, and this the next and the next; and so realize that each thing thus taken hold of is but the agency that takes you each time a step nearer the realization of your fondest ideals. You then hold the key; and bolts that otherwise would remain immovable, by this mighty force, will be thrown before you.

We are born to be neither slaves nor beggars, but to dominion and to plenty. This is our rightful heritage, if we will but recognize and lay claim to it. Many a man and many a woman is to-day longing for conditions better and higher than he or she is in, who might be using the same time now spent in vain, indefinite, spasmodic longings, in putting into operation forces which, accompanied by the right personal activity, would speedily bring the fullest realization of his or her fondest dreams. The great universe is filled with an abundance of all things, filled to overflowing. All there is, is in her, waiting only for the touch of the right forces to cast them forth. She is no respecter of persons outside of the fact that she always responds to the demands of the man or the woman who knows and uses the forces and powers he or she is endowed with. And to the demands of such she always opens her treasure-house, for the supply is always equal to the demand. All things are in the hands of him who knows they are there.

Of all known forms of energy, thought is the most subtle, the most irresistible force. It has always been operating; but, so far as the great masses of the people are concerned, it has been operating blindly, or, rather, they have been blind to its mighty power, except in the cases of a few here and there. And these, as a consequence, have been our prophets, our seers, our sages, our saviors, our men of great and mighty power. We are just beginning to grasp the tremendous truth that there is a *science of thought*, and that the laws governing it can be known and scientifically applied. The man who understands and who appropriates this fact has literally all things under his control. Heredity and its attendant circumstances and influences? you ask. Most surely. The barriers which heredity builds, the same as those environment erects, when the awakened interior forces are considered, are as mud walls standing within the range of a Krupp gun: shattered and crumbled they are when the tremendous force is applied.

Thought needs direction to be effective, and upon this effective results depend as much as upon the force itself. This brings us to the will. Will is not as is so often thought, a force in itself; will is the directing power. Thought is the force. Will gives direction. Thought scattered gives the weak, the uncertain, the vacillating, the aspiring, but the never-doing, the I-would-like-to, but the get-no-where, the attain-to-nothing man or woman. Thought steadily directed by the will, gives the strong, the firm, the never-yielding, the never-know-defeat man or woman, the man or woman who uses the very difficulties and hindrances that would dishearten the ordinary person, as stones with which he paves a way over which he triumphantly walks, who, by the very force he carries with him, so neutralizes and transmutes the very obstacles that would bar his way that they fall before him, and in turn aid him on his way; the man or woman who, like the eagle, uses the very contrary wind that would thwart his flight, that would turn him and carry him in the opposite direction, as the very agency upon which he mounts and mounts and mounts, until actually lost to the human eye, and which, in addition to thus aiding him, brings to him an ever fuller realization of his own powers, or in other words, an ever greater power.

It is this that gives the man or the woman who in storm or in sunny weather, rides over every obstacle, throws before him every barrier, and, as Browning has said, finally "arrives." Take, for example, the successful business man, – for it is all one, the law is the same in all cases, – the man who started with nothing except his own interior equipments. He has made up his mind to *one* thing, – success. This is his ideal. He thinks success, he sees success. He refuses to see anything else. He expects success: he thus attracts it to him, his thought-forces continually attract to him every agency that makes for success. He has set up the current, so that every wind that blows brings him success. He doesn't expect failure, and so he doesn't invite it. He has no time, no energies, to waste in fears or forebodings. He is dauntless, untiring, in his efforts. Let disaster come to-day, and to-morrow – ay, even yet to-day – he is getting his bearings, he is setting forces anew into operation; and these very forces are of more value to him than the half million dollars of his neighbor who has suffered from the same disaster. We speak of a man's failing in business, little thinking that the real failure came long before, and that the final crash is but the culmination, the outward visible manifestation, of the real failure that occurred within possibly long ago. *A man carries his success or his failure with him: it is not dependent upon outside conditions.*

Will is the steady directing power: it is concentration. It is the pilot which, after the vessel is started by the mighty force within, puts it on its right course and keeps it true to that course, the pilot under whose control the rudder is which brings the great ocean liner, even through storms and gales, to an exact spot in the Liverpool port within a few minutes of its scheduled time, and at times even upon the very minute. Will is the sun-glass which so concentrates and so focuses the sun's rays that they quickly burn a hole through the paper that is held before it. The same rays, not thus concentrated, not thus focused, would fall upon the paper for days without any effect whatever. Will is the means for the directing, the concentrating, the focusing, of the thought-forces. Thought under wise direction, – this it is that does the work, that brings results, that makes the successful career. One object in mind which we never lose sight of; an ideal steadily held before the mind, never lost sight of, never lowered, never swerved from, – this, with persistence, determines all. Nothing can resist the power of thought, when thus directed by will.

May not this power, then, be used for base as well as for good purposes, for selfish as well as for unselfish ends? The same with this modification, – the more highly thought is spiritualized, the more subtle and powerful it becomes; and the more highly spiritualized the life, the farther is it removed from base, ignoble, self-ish ends. But, even if it can be thus used, let him who would so use it be careful, let him never forget that that mighty, searching, omnipotent law of the right, of truth, of justice, that runs through all the universe and that can never be annulled or even for a moment set aside, will drive him to the wall, will crush him with a terrific force if he so use it.

Let him never forget that whatever he may get for self at the expense of some one else, through deception, through misrepresentation, through the exercise of the lower functions and powers, will by a law equally subtle, equally powerful, be turned into ashes in his very hands. The honey he thinks he has secured will be turned into bitterness as he attempts to eat it; the beautiful fruit he thinks is his will be as wormwood as he tries to enjoy it; the rose he has plucked will vanish, and he will find himself clutching a handful of thorns, which will penetrate to the very quick and which will flow the very life-blood from his hands. For through the violation of a higher, an immutable law, though he may get this or that, the power of true enjoyment will be taken away, and what he gets will become as a thorn in his side: either this or it will sooner or later escape from his hands. God's triumphal-car moves in a direction and at a rate that is certain and absolute, and he who would oppose it or go contrary to it must fall and be crushed beneath its wheels; and for him this crushing is necessary, in order that it may bring him the more quickly to a knowledge of the higher laws, to a realization of the higher self.

This brings to our notice two orders of will, which we may term, for convenience' sake, the human and the divine. The human will is the one just noticed, the sense will, the will of the lower self, that which seeks its own ends regardless of its connection with the greater whole. The divine will is the will of the higher self, the god-self, that that never makes an error, that never leads into difficulties. How attain to its realization? How call it into a dominating activity? Through an awakening to and a living in the higher, the god-self, thus making it one with God's will, one with the will of infinite intelligence, infinite love, infinite wisdom, infinite power; and when this is done, no mistakes can be made, any more than limits can be set.

It is thus that the Infinite Power works through and for us – true inspiration – while our part is simply to see that our connection with this power is consciously and perfectly kept. And, when we come to a knowledge of the true nature, a knowledge of the true self, when we come to a conscious realization of the fact that we are one with, a part of, this spirit of infinite life, infinite love, infinite wisdom, infinite power, and infinite plenty, do we not see that we lack for nothing, that all things *are* ours? It is then ours to speak the word: desire induces and gives place to realization. If you are intelligence, if you are power, if you are that all-seeing, all-knowing, all-doing, all-loving, all-having, that eternal self, that eternal one without beginning and without end, the same yesterday, to-day, and forever, then all things *are* yours, and you lack for nothing; and, when you come consciously to know and to live this truth, then the whole of life for you is summed up in the one word *realization*. The striving, the pulling, the running hither and thither to accomplish this or that, that takes place on all planes of life below this highest plane, gives place to this *realization;* and you and your desire become one.

And what does this mean? Simply this: that you have found and have literally entered into the kingdom of heaven, and heaven means harmony, so that you have entered into the kingdom of harmony, – harmony or oneness with the Infinite Life, the Infinite God. And do we not, then, clearly see the rational and scientific basis for the injunction – seek ye first the kingdom of heaven, and all these other things shall be added unto you? Than this there is nothing in all the wide universe more scientific, nothing more practical; and in the light of this can we not also see how readily follows the injunction – Take ye no thought for the things of the morrow, for the things of the morrow will take care of themselves? This realization gives you that care-less attitude, free from care. The Infinite Power does the work for you, and you are relieved of the responsibility. Your responsibility lies in keeping yourself in a faithful and a never-failing connection with this Infinite Source. Why, I know a few lives that have come into such a conscious one-ness with the Infinite Life, and who so continually live in its realization, that all things that have just been said are *absolutely* true in their cases. The solution of all things they thus put into the law, so that, when the time comes, the difficulty is solved, the course is clear, the way is opened, or the means are at hand. When one knows whereof he speaks, of this he can speak with authority.

When this realization comes, fear goes, hope attends, faith dominates, – the faith of to-day which gives place to the realization of to-morrow. We then have nothing to do with the past, nothing to do with the future; for the whole of life is determined by the ever-present to-day. As my life to-day has been determined by the way I lived my yesterday, so my to-morrow is being determined by the way I live my to-day. Let me then live in this *eternal now*, and realize that I am at this very moment living the eternal life as much as I ever shall or can live it. I will then waste no time with the past, except perhaps occasionally to give thanks that its then seeming trials, sorrows, errors, and stumblings have brought me all the sooner into harmony with the laws of the higher life. Let me waste no time with the future, no time in idle dreaming, neither in fears nor forebodings, thus inviting and opening the door for the entrance of their actualizations; but rather let me, by the thoughts and so by the deeds of to-day, make the future exactly what I will.

Every act is preceded and given birth to by a thought, the act repeated forms the habit, the habit determines the character, and character determines the life, the destiny, – a most significant, a most tremendous truth: thought on the one hand, life, destiny, on the other. And how simplified, when we realize that it is merely the thought of the present hour, and the next when it comes, and the next, and the next! so life, destiny, on the one hand, the thoughts of the present hour, on the other. This is the secret of character-building. How wonderfully simple, though what vigilance it demands!

What, shall we ask, is the place, what the value, of prayer? Prayer, as every act of devotion, brings us into an ever greater conscious harmony with the Infinite, the one pearl of great price; for it is this harmony which brings all other things. Prayer is the soul's sincere desire, and thus is its own answer, as the sincere desire made active and accompanied by faith sooner or later gives place to realization; *for faith is an invisible and invincible magnet, and attracts to itself whatever it fervently desires and calmly and persistently expects.* This is absolute, and the results will be absolute in exact proportion as this operation of the thought forces, as this faith is absolute, and relative in exact proportion as it is relative. The Master said, What things soever ye desire, when ye pray, *believe* that ye receive them and ye shall have them. Can any law be more clearly enunciated, can anything be more definite and more absolute than this? According to thy faith be it unto thee. Do we at times fail in obtaining the results we desire? The fault, the failure, lies not in the law but in ourselves. Regarded in its right and true light, than prayer there is nothing more scientific, nothing more valuable, nothing more effective.

This conscious realization of oneness with the Infinite Life is of all things the one thing to be desired; for, when this oneness is realized and lived in, all other things follow in its train, there are no desires that shall not be realized, for God has planted in the human breast no desire without its corresponding means of realization. No harm can come nigh, nothing can touch us, there will be nothing to fear; for we shall thus attract only the good. And whatever changes time may bring, understanding the law, we shall always expect something better, and thus set into operation the forces that will attract that something, realizing that many times angels go out that arch-angels may enter in; and this is always true in the case of the life of this higher realization. And why should we have any fear whatever, – fear even for the nation, as is many times expressed? God is behind His world, in love and with infinite care and watchfulness working out his great and almighty plans; and whatever plans men may devise, He will when the time is ripe either frustrate and shatter, or aid and push through to their most perfect culmination, – frustrate and shatter if contrary to, aid and actualize if in harmony with His.

It will readily be seen what a power the life that is fully awake, that fully grasps and uses the great forces of its own interior self, can be in the service of mankind. One with these forces highly spiritualized will not have to go here and there to do the greatest service for mankind. Such a one can sit in his cabin, in his tent, in his own home, or, as he goes here and there, he can continually send out influences of the most potent and powerful nature, – influences that will have their effect, that will do their work, and that will reach to the uttermost parts of the world. Than this there can be no more valuable, more vital service, nor one of a higher nature.

These facts, the facts relating to the powers that come with the higher awakening, have been dealt with somewhat fully, to show that the matters along the lines of man's interior, intuitive, spiritual, thought, soul life, instead of being, as they are so many times regarded, merely indefinite, sentimental, or impractical, are, on the contrary, powerfully, omnipotently real, and are of all practical things in the world the most practical, and, in the truest and deepest sense, the only truly practical things there are. And pre-eminently is this true when we look with a long range of vision, past the mere to-day, to the final outcome, to the time when that transition we are accustomed to call death takes place, and all accumulations and possessions material are left behind, and the soul takes with it only the unfoldment and growth of the real life; and unless it has this, when all else must be left behind, it goes out poor indeed. And a most wonderful and beautiful fact of it all is this: that all growth, all advancement, all attainment made along the lines of the spiritual, the soul, the real life, is so much made forever, and can never be lost. Hence the great fact in the admonition, Lay not up for yourselves treasures on earth, where moth doth corrupt and where thieves break through and steal; but lay up for yourselves treasures in heaven, – the interior, spiritual kingdom, – where neither moth doth corrupt nor where thieves break through and steal.

What then, again let us ask, is love to God? It is far more, we have found, than a mere sentimental abstraction. It is this awakening to the higher, the god-self, a coming into the conscious realization of the fact that your life is one with, is a part of, the Infinite Life, the full realization of the fact that you are a spiritual being here and now, at this very moment, and a living as such. It is being true to the light that lighteth every man that cometh into the world, and so a finding of the Christ within; a realization of the fact that God is the life of your life, and so not afar off; a realization of a oneness so perfect that you are able to say, as did His other son, "I and my Father are one" – the ultimate destiny of each human soul, each of the Father's children, for all, no matter what differences man may see, are equal in His sight; and He created not one in vain. So love to God in its true expression is not a mere sentimentality, a mere abstraction: it is life, it is growth, it is spiritual awakening and unfoldment, it is realization. Again, it is life: it is the more abundant life.

Then recognize this fact, and so fill your life with an intense, a passionate love for God. Then take this life, so rich, so abundant, and so powerful, and lose it in the love and service of your fellow-men, the Father's other children. Fill it with an intense, a passionate love for service; and when this shall have been done, your life is in complete harmony with all the law and the prophets, in complete harmony with the two great and determining facts of human life and destiny, – love to God and love to one's fellow-men, – the two eternal principles upon which the great universal religion, which is slowly and gradually evolving out an almost endless variety and form, is to rest. Do this, and feel once for all the power and the thrill of the life universal. Do this, and find yourself coming into the full realization of such splendors and beauties as all the royal courts of this world combined have never been able even to dream of.

When the step from the personal to the impersonal, from the personal, the individual, to the universal, is once made, the great solution of life has come; and by this same step one enters at once into the realm of all power. When this is done, and one fully realizes the fact that the greatest life is the life spent in the service of all mankind, and then when he vitally grasps that great eternal principle of right, of truth, of justice, that runs through all the universe, and which, though temporarily it may seem to be perverted, always and with never an exception eventually prevails, and that with an omnipotent power, – he then holds the key to all situations.

A king of this nature goes about his work absolutely regardless of what men may say or hear or think or do; for he himself has absolutely nothing to gain or nothing to lose, and nothing of this nature can come near him or touch him, for he is standing not in the personal, but in the universal. He is then in God's work, and the very God-powers are his, and it seems as if the very angels of heaven come to minister unto him and to move things his way; and this is true, very true, for he himself is simply moving God's way, and when this is so, the certainty of the outcome is absolute.

How often did the Master say, "I seek not to do mine own will, but the will of the Father who sent me"! Here is the world's great example of the life out of the personal and in the universal, hence his great power. The same has been true of all the saviors, the prophets, the seers, the sages, and the leaders in the world's history, of all of truly great and lasting power.

He who would then come into the secret of power must come from the personal into the universal, and with this comes not only great power, but also freedom from the vexations and perplexities that rise from the misconstruing of motives, the opinions of others; for such a one cares nothing as to what men may say, or hear, or think, or do, so long as he is true to the great principles of right and truth before him. And, if we will search carefully, we shall find that practically all the perplexities and difficulties of life have their origin on the side of the personal.

Much is said to young men to-day about success in life, – success generally though, as the world calls success. It is well, however, always to bear in mind the fact that there is a success which is a miserable, a deplorable failure; while, on the other hand, there is a failure which is a grand, a noble, a God-like success. And one crying need of the age is that young men be taught the true dignity, nobility, and power of such a failure, – such a failure in the eyes of the world to-day, but such a success in the eyes of God and the coming ages. When this is done, there will be among us more prophets, more saviors, more men of grand and noble stature, who with a firm and steady hand will hold the lighted torch of true advancement high up among the people; and they will be those whom the people will gladly follow, for they will be those who will speak and move with authority, true sons of God, true brothers of men. A man may make his millions and his life be a failure still.

❧

The promise was given that our conversation should not be extended; and unless we conclude it now, the promise will not be kept. Our aim at the outset, you will remember, was to find answer to the question – How can I make life yield its fullest and best? how can I know the true secret of power? how can I attain to true greatness? how can I fill the whole of life with a happiness, a peace, a joy, a satisfaction, that is ever rich and abiding, that ever increases, never diminishes?

Two great laws come forward: the one, that we find our own lives in losing them in the service of others, – love to the fellow-man; the other, that all life is one with, is part of, the Infinite Life, that we are not material, but spiritual beings, – spiritual beings here and now, and a living as such, which brings us in turn to a realization of the higher, the god-self, thus bringing us into the realm of all peace, all power, and all plenty, – this is love to God.

And I wonder now if we have found the answer true and satisfactory. We have sat at the feet of the Master Teacher, and he has told us that we have. We have found that through them, and through them alone, *true* greatness, power, and success can come; that through them comes the richest joy, the greatest peace and satisfaction this world can know. We have also found that, if one's desire is to make life narrow, pinched, and of little value, to rob it of its chief charms, the only requirement necessary is to become self-centred, to live continually with the little, stunted self, which will inevitably grow more and more diminutive and shrivelled as time passes, instead of reaching out and having a part in the great life of humanity, thus illimitably intensifying and multiplying his own. For each act of humble service is that divine touching of the ground which enables one to get the spring whereby he leaps to ever greater heights. We have found that a recognition of these two laws enables one to grow and develop the fullest and richest life here, and that they are the two gates whereby all who would must enter the kingdom of heaven.

Around this great and sweet-incensed altar of love, service, and self-devotion to God and the fellow-man, can and do all mankind bow and worship. To it can all religions and creeds subscribe: it is the universal religion.

Then become at one with God, as did His other son, through the awakening to the real self and by living continually in this the higher, the god-self. Become at one with humanity, as did His other son, by bringing your life into harmony with this great, immutable law of love and service and self-devotion, and so feel once for all the power and the thrill of the life universal.

Yours will then be a life the greatest, the grandest, the most joyous this world can know; for you will indeed be living the Christ-life, the life that is beyond compare, the life to which all the world stretches out its eager palms, and innumerable companies will rise up and call you blessed, and give thanks that such a life is the rich heritage of the world. The song continually arising from your lips will then be, There is joy, only joy; for we are all one with the Infinite Life, all parts of the one great whole, and the Spirit of Infinite Goodness and Love is ever ruling over all.

PART VI

CHARACTER-BUILDING THOUGHT POWER

A thought, – good or evil, – an act, in time a habit, – so runs life's law: what you live in your thought-world, that, sooner or later, you will find objectified in your life.

UNCONSCIOUSLY we are forming habits every moment of our lives. Some are habits of a desirable nature; some are those of a most undesirable nature. Some, though not so bad in themselves, are exceedingly bad in their cumulative effects, and cause us at times much loss, much pain and anguish, while their opposites would, on the contrary, bring us much peace and joy, as well as a continually increasing power.

Have we it within our power to determine at all times what types of habits shall take form in our lives? In other words, is habit-forming, character-building, a matter of mere chance, or have we it within our own control? We have, entirely and absolutely. "I will be what I will to be," can be said and should be said by every human soul.

After this has been bravely and determinedly said, and not only said, but fully inwardly realized, something yet remains. Something remains to be said regarding the great law underlying habit-forming, character-building; for there is a simple, natural, and thoroughly scientific method that all should know. A method whereby old, undesirable, earth-binding habits can be broken, and new, desirable, heaven-lifting habits can be acquired, – a method whereby life in part or in its totality can be changed, provided one is sufficiently in earnest to know, and, knowing it, to apply the law.

Thought is the force underlying all. And what do we mean by this? Simply this: Your every act – every conscious act – is preceded by a thought. Your dominating thoughts determine your dominating actions. The acts repeated crystallize themselves into the habit. The aggregate of your habits is your character. Whatever, then, you would have your acts, you must look well to the character of the thought you entertain. Whatever act you would not do, – habit you would not acquire, – you must look well to it that you do not entertain the type of thought that will give birth to this act, this habit.

It is a simple psychological law that any type of thought, if entertained for a sufficient length of time, will, by and by, reach the motor tracks of the brain, and finally burst forth into action. Murder can be and many times is committed in this way, the same as all undesirable things are done. On the other hand, the greatest powers are grown, the most God-like characteristics are engendered, the most heroic acts are performed in the same way.

The thing clearly to understand is this: That the thought is always parent to the act. Now, we have it entirely in our own hands to determine exactly what thoughts we entertain. In the realm of our own minds we have absolute control, or we should have, and if at any time we have not, then there is a method by which we can gain control, and in the realm of the mind become thorough masters. In order to get to the very foundation of the matter, let us look to this for a moment. For if thought is always parent to our acts, habits, character, life, then it is first necessary that we know fully how to control our thoughts.

Here let us refer to that law of the mind which is the same as is the law in connection with the reflex nerve system of the body, the law which says that whenever one does a certain thing in a certain way it is easier to do the same thing in the same way the next time, and still easier the next, and the next, and the next, until in time it comes to pass that no effort is required, or no effort worth speaking of; but on the contrary, to do the opposite would require the effort. The mind carries with it the power that perpetuates its own type of thought, the same as the body carries with it through the reflex nerve system the power which perpetuates and makes continually easier its own particular acts. Thus a simple effort to control one's thoughts, a simple setting about it, even if at first failure is the result, and even if for a time failure seems to be about the only result, will in time, sooner or later, bring him to the point of easy, full, and complete control.

Each one, then, can grow the power of determining, controlling his thought, the power of determining what types of thought he shall and what types he shall not entertain. For let us never part in mind with this fact, that every earnest *effort* along any line makes the end aimed at just a little easier for each succeeding effort, even if, as has been said, apparent failure is the result of the earlier efforts. This is a case where even failure is success, for the failure is not in the effort, and every earnest effort adds an increment of power that will eventually accomplish the end aimed at. We *can,* then, gain the full and complete power of determining what character, what type of thoughts we entertain.

Shall we now give attention to some two or three concrete cases? Here is a man, the cashier of a large mercantile establishment, or cashier of a bank. In his morning paper he reads of a man who has become suddenly rich, has made a fortune of half a million or a million dollars in a few hours through speculation on the stock market. Perhaps he has seen an account of another man who has done practically the same thing lately. He is not quite wise enough, however, to comprehend the fact that when he reads of one or two cases of this kind he could find, were he to look into the matter carefully, one or two hundred cases of men who have lost all they had in the same way. He thinks, however, that he will be one of the fortunate ones. He does not fully realize that there are no short cuts to wealth honestly made. He takes a part of his savings, and as is true in practically all cases of this kind, he loses all that he has put in. Thinking now that he sees why he lost, and that had he more money he would be able to get back what he has lost, and perhaps make a handsome sum in addition, and make it quickly, the thought comes to him to use some of the funds he has charge of. In nine cases out of ten, if not in ten cases in every ten, the results that inevitably follow this are known sufficiently well to make it unnecessary to follow him farther. Where is the man's safety in the light of what we have been considering? Simply this: the moment the thought of using for his own purpose funds belonging to others enters his mind, if he is wise he will *instantly* put the thought from his mind. If he is a fool he will entertain it. In the degree in which he entertains it, it will grow upon him; it will become the absorbing thought in his mind; it will finally become master of his will power, and through rapidly succeeding steps, dishonor, shame, degradation, penitentiary, remorse will be his. It is easy for him to put the thought from his mind when it first enters; but as he entertains it, it grows into such proportions that it becomes more and more difficult for him to put it from his mind; and by and by it becomes practically *impossible* for him to do it. The light of the match, which but a little effort of the breath would have extinguished at first, has imparted a flame that is raging through the entire building, and now it is almost, if not quite impossible to conquer it.

Shall we notice another concrete case? a trite case, perhaps, but one in which we can see how habit is formed, and also how the same habit can be unformed. Here is a young man, he may be the son of poor parents, or he may be the son of rich parents; one in the ordinary ranks of life, or one of high social standing, whatever that means. He is good-hearted, one of good impulses, generally speaking, – a good fellow. He is out with some companions, companions of the same general type. They are out for a pleasant evening, out for a good time. They are apt at times to be thoughtless, even careless. The suggestion is made by one of the company, not that they get drunk, no, not at all; but merely that they go and have something to drink together. The young man whom we first mentioned, wanting to be genial, scarcely listens to the suggestion that comes to his inner consciousness – that it will be better for him not to fall in with the others in this. He does not stop long enough to realize the fact that the greatest strength and nobility of character lies always in taking a firm stand on the side of the right, and allow himself to be influenced by nothing that will weaken this stand. He goes, therefore, with his companions to the drinking place. With the same or with other companions this is repeated now and then; and each time it is repeated his power of saying "No" is gradually decreasing. In this way he has grown a little liking for intoxicants, and takes them perhaps now and then by himself. He does not dream, or in the slightest degree realize, what way he is tending, until there comes a day when he wakens to the consciousness of the fact that he hasn't the power nor even the impulse to resist the taste which has gradually grown into a minor form of craving for intoxicants. Thinking, however, that he will be able to stop when he is really in danger of getting into the drink habit, he goes thoughtlessly and carelessly on. We will pass over the various intervening steps and come to the time when we find him a confirmed drunkard. It is simply the same old story told a thousand or even a million times over.

He finally awakens to his true condition; and through the shame, the anguish, the degradation, and the want that comes upon him he longs for a return of the days when he was a free man. But hope has almost gone from his life. It would have been easier for him never to have begun, and easier for him to have stopped before he reached his present condition, but even in his present condition, be it the lowest and the most helpless and hopeless that can be imagined, he has the power to get out of it and be a free man once again. Let us see. The desire for drink comes upon him again. If he entertain the thought, the desire, he is lost again. His only hope, his only means of escape is this: the moment, aye, *the very instant* the thought comes to him, if he will put it out of his mind he will thereby put out the little flame of the match. If he entertain the thought the little flame will communicate itself until almost before he is aware of it a consuming fire is raging, and then effort is almost useless. The thought must be banished from the mind the instant it enters; dalliance with it means failure and defeat, or a fight that will be indescribably fiercer than it would be if the thought is ejected at the beginning.

And here we must say a word regarding a certain great law that we may call the "law of indirectness." A thought can be put out of the mind easier and more successfully, not by dwelling upon it, not by attempting to put it out *directly*, but by throwing the mind on to some other object, by putting some other object of thought into the mind. This may be, for example, the ideal of full and perfect self-mastery, or it may be something of a nature entirely distinct from the thought which presents itself, something to which the mind goes easily and naturally. This will in time become the absorbing thought in the mind, and the danger is past. This same course of action repeated, will gradually grow the power of putting more readily out of mind the thought of drink as it presents itself, and will gradually grow the power of putting into the mind those objects of thought one most desires. The result will be that as time passes the thought of drink will present itself less and less, and when it does present itself it can be put out of the mind more easily each succeeding time, until the time comes when it can be put out without difficulty, and eventually the time will come when the thought will enter the mind no more at all.

Still another case. You may be more or less of an irritable nature – naturally, perhaps, provoked easily to anger. Some one says something or does something that you dislike, and your first impulse is to show resentment and possibly to give way to anger. In the degree that you allow this resentment to display itself, that you allow yourself to give way to anger, in that degree will it become easier to do the same thing when any cause, even a very slight cause, presents itself. It will, moreover, become continually harder for you to refrain from it, until resentment, anger, and possibly even hatred and revenge become characteristics of your nature, robbing it of its sunniness, its charm, and its brightness for all with whom you come in contact. If, however, the instant the impulse to resentment and anger arises, you check it *then and there,* and throw the mind on to some other object of thought, the power will gradually grow itself of doing this same thing more readily, more easily, as succeeding like causes present themselves, until by and by the time will come when there will be scarcely anything that can irritate you, and nothing that can impel you to anger; until by and by a matchless brightness and charm of nature and disposition will become habitually yours, a brightness and charm you would scarcely think possible to-day. And so we might take up case after case, characteristic after characteristic, habit after habit. The habit of fault-finding and its opposite are grown in identically the same way; the characteristic of jealousy and its opposite; the characteristic of fear and its opposite. In this same way we grow either love or hatred; in this way we come to take a gloomy, pessimistic view of life, which objectifies itself in a nature, a disposition of this type, or we grow that sunny, hopeful, cheerful, buoyant nature that brings with it so much joy and beauty and power for ourselves, as well as so much hope and inspiration and joy for all the world.

There is nothing more true in connection with human life than that we grow into the likeness of those things we contemplate. Literally and scientifically and necessarily true is it that, "as a man thinketh in his heart, so *is* he." The "is" part is his character. His character is the sum total of his habits. His habits have been formed by his conscious acts; but every conscious act is, as we have found, preceded by a thought. And so we have it – thought on the one hand, character, life, destiny on the other. And simple it becomes when we bear in mind that it is simply the thought of the present moment, and the next moment when it is upon us, and then the next, and so on through all time.

One can in this way attain to whatever ideals he would attain to. Two steps are necessary: first, as the days pass, to form one's ideals; and second, to follow them continually whatever may arise, wherever they may lead him. Always remember that the great and strong character is the one who is ever ready to sacrifice the present pleasure for the future good. He who will thus follow his highest ideals as they present themselves to him day after day, year after year, will find that as Dante, following his beloved from world to world, finally found her at the gates of Paradise, so he will find himself eventually at the same gates. Life is not, we may say, for mere passing pleasure, but for the highest unfoldment that one can attain to, the noblest character that one can grow, and for the greatest service that one can render to all mankind. In this, however, we will find the highest pleasure, for in this the only real pleasure lies. He who would find it by any short cuts, or by entering upon any other paths, will inevitably find that his last state is always worse than his first; and if he proceed upon paths other than these he will find that he will never find real and lasting pleasure at all. The question is not, What are the conditions in our lives? but, How do we meet the conditions that we find there? And whatever the conditions are, it is unwise and profitless to look upon them, even if they are conditions that we would have otherwise, in the attitude of complaint, for complaint will bring depression, and depression will weaken and possibly even kill the spirit that would engender the power that would enable us to bring into our lives an entirely new set of conditions.

In order to be concrete, even at the risk of being personal, I will say that in my own experience there have come at various times into my life circumstances and conditions that I gladly would have run from at the time – conditions that caused at the time humiliation and shame and anguish of spirit. But invariably, as sufficient time has passed, I have been able to look back and see clearly the part which every experience of the type just mentioned had to play in my life. I have seen the lessons it was essential for me to learn; and the result is that now I would not drop a single one of these experiences from my life, humiliating and hard to bear as they were at the time; no, not for the world. And here is also a lesson I have learned: whatever conditions are in my life to-day that are not the easiest and most agreeable, and whatever conditions of this type all coming time may bring, I will take them just as they come, without complaint, without depression, and meet them in the wisest possible way; knowing that they are the best possible conditions that could be in my life at the time, or otherwise they would not be there; realizing the fact that, although I may not at the time see why they are in my life, although I may not see just what part they have to play, the time will come, and when it comes I will see it all, and thank God for every condition just as it came.

Each one is so apt to think that his own conditions, his own trials or troubles or sorrows, or his own struggles, as the case may be, are greater than those of the great mass of mankind, or possibly greater than those of anyone else in the world. He forgets that each one has his own peculiar trials or troubles or borrows to bear, or struggles in habits to overcome, and that his is but the common lot of all the human race. We are apt to make the mistake in this – in that we see and feel keenly our own trials, or adverse conditions, or characteristics to be overcome, while those of others we do not see so clearly, and hence we are apt to think that they are not at all equal to our own. Each has his own problems to work out. Each must work out his own problems. Each must grow the insight that will enable him to see what the causes are that have brought the unfavorable conditions into his life; each must grow the strength that will enable him to face these conditions, and to set into operation forces that will bring about a different set of conditions. We may be of aid to one another by way of suggestion, by way of bringing to one another a knowledge of certain higher laws and forces, – laws and forces that will make it easier to do that which we would do. The doing, however, must be done by each one for himself.

And so the way to get out of any conditions we have gotten into, either knowingly or inadvertently, either intentionally or unintentionally, is to take time to look the conditions squarely in the face, and to find the law whereby they have come about. And when we have discovered the law, the thing to do is not to rebel against it, not to resist it, but to go with it by working in harmony with it. If we work in harmony with it, it will work for our highest good, and will take us wheresoever we desire. If we oppose it, if we resist it, if we fail to work in harmony with it, it will eventually break us to pieces. The law is immutable in its workings. Go with it, and it brings all things our way; resist it, and it brings suffering, pain, loss, and desolation.

But a few days ago I was talking with a lady, a most estimable lady living on a little New England farm of some five or six acres. Her husband died a few years ago, a good-hearted, industrious man, but one who spent practically all of his earnings in drink. When he died the little farm was unpaid for, and the wife found herself without any visible means of support, with a family of several to care for. Instead of being discouraged with what many would have called her hard lot, instead of rebelling against the circumstances in which she found herself, she faced the matter bravely, firmly believing that there were ways by which she could manage, though she could not see them clearly at the time. She took up her burden where she found it, and went bravely forward. For several years she has been taking care of summer boarders who come to that part of the country, getting up regularly, she told me, at from half-past three to four o'clock in the morning, and working until ten o'clock each night. In the winter-time, when this means of revenue is cut off, she has gone out to do nursing in the country round about. In this way the little farm is now almost paid for; her children have been kept in school, and they are now able to aid her to a greater or less extent. Through it all she has entertained no fears nor forebodings; she has shown no rebellion of any kind. She has not kicked against the circumstances which brought about the conditions in which she found herself, but she has put herself into harmony with the law that would bring her into another set of conditions. And through it all, she told me, she had been continually grateful that she has been able to work, and that whatever her own circumstances have been, she has never yet failed to find some one whose circumstances were still a little worse than hers, and for whom it was not possible for her to render some little service.

Most heartily she appreciates the fact, and most grateful is she for it, that the little home is now almost paid for, and soon no more of her earnings will have to go out in that channel. The dear little home, she said, would be all the more precious to her by virtue of the fact that it was finally hers through her own efforts. The strength and nobility of character that have come to her during these years, the sweetness of disposition, the sympathy and care for others, her faith in the final triumph of all that is honest and true and pure and good, are qualities that thousands and hundreds of thousands of women, yes, of both men and women, who are apparently in better circumstances in life can justly envy. And should the little farm home be taken away to-morrow, she has gained something that a farm of a thousand acres could not buy. By going about her work in the way she has gone about it the burden of it all has been lightened, and her work has been made truly enjoyable.

Let us take a moment to see how these same conditions would have been met by a person of less wisdom, one not so far-sighted as this dear, good woman has been. For a time possibly her spirit would have been crushed. Fears and forebodings of all kinds would probably have taken hold of her, and she would have felt that nothing that she could do would be of any avail. Or, she might have rebelled against the agencies, against the law which brought about the conditions in which she found herself, and she might have become embittered against the world, and gradually also against the various people with whom she came in contact. Or again, she might have thought that her efforts would be unable to meet the circumstances, and that it was the duty of some one to lift her out of her difficulties. In this way no progress at all would have been made towards the accomplishment of the desired results, and continually she would have felt more keenly the circumstances in which she found herself, because there was nothing else to occupy her mind. In this way the little farm would not have become hers, she would not have been able to do anything for others, and her nature would have become embittered against everything and everybody.

True it is, then, not, What are the conditions in one's life? but, How does he meet the conditions that he finds there? This will determine all. And if at any time we are apt to think that our own lot is about the hardest there is, and if we are able at any time to persuade ourselves that we can find no one whose lot is just a little harder than ours, let us then study for a little while the character Pompilia, in Browning's poem,[4] and after studying it, thank God that the conditions in our life are so favorable; and then set about with a trusting and intrepid spirit to actualize the conditions that we most desire.

෴

Thought is at the bottom of all progress or retrogression, of all success or failure, of all that is desirable or undesirable in human life. The type of thought we entertain both creates and draws conditions that crystallize about it, conditions exactly the same in nature as is the thought that gives them form. Thoughts are forces, and each creates of its kind, whether we realize it or not. The great law of the drawing power of the mind, which says that like creates like, and that like attracts like, is continually working in every human life, for it is one of the great immutable laws of the universe. For one to take time to see clearly the things he would attain to, and then to hold that ideal steadily and continually before his mind, never allowing faith – his positive thought-forces – to give way to or to be neutralized by doubts and fears, and then to set about doing each day what his hands find to do, never complaining, but spending the time that he would otherwise spend in complaint in focusing his thought-forces upon the ideal that his mind has built, will sooner or later bring about the full materialization of that for which he sets out.

There are those who, when they begin to grasp the fact that there is what we may term a "science of thought," who, when they begin to realize that through the instrumentality of our interior, spiritual thought-forces we have the power of gradually moulding the every-day conditions of life as we would have them, in their early enthusiasm are not able to see results as quickly as they expect, and are apt to think, therefore, that after all there is not very much in that which has but newly come to their knowledge. They must remember, however, that in endeavoring to overcome an old or to grow a new habit, everything cannot be done *all at once*.

In the degree that we attempt to use the thought-forces do we continually become able to use them more effectively. Progress is slow at first, more rapid as we proceed. Power grows by using, or, in other words, using brings a continually increasing power. This

---

4   "The Ring and the Book," by Robert Browning.

is governed by law the same as are all things in our lives, and all things in the universe about us. Every act and advancement made by the musician is in full accordance with law. No one commencing the study of music can, for example, sit down to the piano and play the piece of a master at the first effort. He must not conclude, however, nor does he conclude, that the piece of the master *cannot be* played by him, or, for that matter, by any one. He begins to practise the piece. The law of the mind that we have already noticed comes to his aid, whereby his mind follows the music more readily, more rapidly, and more surely each succeeding time, and there also comes into operation and to his aid the law underlying the action of the reflex nerve system of the body, which we have also noticed, whereby his fingers coordinate their movements with the movements of his mind, more readily, more rapidly, and more accurately each succeeding time; until by and by the time comes when that which he stumbles through at first, that in which there is no harmony, nothing but discord, finally reveals itself as the music of the master, the music that thrills and moves masses of men and women. So it is in the use of the thought-forces. It is the reiteration, the constant reiteration of the thought that grows the power of continually stronger thought-focusing, and that finally brings manifestation.

∾

All life is from within out. This is something that cannot be reiterated too often. The springs of life are all from within. This being true, it would be well for us to give more time to the inner life than we are accustomed to give to it, especially in this Western world.

There is nothing that will bring us such abundant returns as to take a little time in the quiet each day of our lives. We need this to get the kinks out of our minds and hence out of our lives. We need this to form better the higher ideals of life. We need this in order to see clearly in mind the things upon which we would concentrate and focus the thought-forces. We need this in order to make continually anew and to keep our conscious connection with the Infinite. We need this in order that the rush and hurry of our every-day life does not keep us away from the conscious realization of the fact that the spirit of Infinite life and power that is back of all, working in and through all, the life of all, is the life of our life, and the source of our power; and that outside of this we have no life and we have no power. To realize this fact fully, and to live in it consciously at all times, is to find the kingdom of God, which is essentially an inner kingdom, and can never be anything else. The kingdom of heaven is to be found only within, and this is done once for all, and in a manner in which it cannot otherwise be done, when we come into the conscious, living realization of the fact that in our real selves we are essentially one with the Divine life, and open ourselves continually so that this Divine life can speak to and manifest through us. In this way we come into the condition where we are continually walking with God. In this way the consciousness of God becomes a living reality in our lives; and in the degree in which it becomes a reality does it bring us into the realization of continually increasing wisdom, insight, and power. *This consciousness of God in the soul of man is the essence, indeed the sum and substance of all religion.* This identifies religion with every act and every moment of everyday life. That which does not identify itself with every moment of every day and with every act of life is religion in name only and not in reality. This consciousness of God in the soul of man is the one thing uniformly taught by all the prophets, by all the inspired ones, by all the seers and mystics in the world's history, whatever the time, wherever the country, whatever the religion, whatever minor differences we may find in their lives and teachings. In regard to this they all agree; indeed, this is the essence of their teaching, as it has also been the secret of their power and the secret of their lasting influence.

It is the attitude of the child that is necessary before we can enter into the kingdom of heaven. As it was said, "Except ye become as little children, ye cannot enter into the kingdom of heaven." For we then realize that of ourselves we can do nothing, but that it is only as we realize that it is the Divine life and power working within us, and it is only as we open ourselves that it may work through us, that we are or can do anything. It is thus that the simple life, which is essentially the life of the greatest enjoyment and the greatest attainment, is entered upon.

In the Orient the people as a class take far more time in the quiet, in the silence, than we take. Some of them carry this possibly to as great an extreme as we carry the opposite, with the result that they do not actualize and objectify in the outer life the things they dream in the inner life. We give so much time to the activities of the outer life that we do not take sufficient time in the quiet to form in the inner, spiritual thought-life the ideals and the conditions that we would have actualized and manifested in the outer life. The result is that we take life in a kind of haphazard way, taking it as it comes, thinking not very much about it until, perhaps, pushed by some bitter experiences, instead of moulding it, through the agency of the inner forces, exactly as we would have it. We need to strike the happy balance between the custom in this respect of the Eastern and Western worlds, and go to the extreme of neither the one nor the other. This alone will give the ideal life; and it is the ideal life only that is the thoroughly satisfactory life. In the Orient there are many who are day after day sitting in the quiet, meditating, contemplating, idealizing, with their eyes focused on their stomach in spiritual revery, while through lack of outer activities, in their stomachs they are actually starving. In this Western world, men and women, in the rush and activity of our accustomed life, are running hither and thither, with no centre, no foundation upon which to stand, nothing to which they can anchor their lives, because they do not take sufficient time to come into the realization of what the centre, of what the reality of their lives is.

If the Oriental would do his contemplating, and then get up and do his work, he would be in a better condition; he would be living a more normal and satisfactory life. If we in the Occident would take more time from the rush and activity of life for contemplation, for meditation, for idealization, for becoming acquainted with our real selves, and then go about our work manifesting the powers of our real selves, we would be far better off, because we would be living a more natural, a more normal life. To find one's centre, to become centred in the Infinite, is the first great essential of every satisfactory life; and then to go out, thinking, speaking, working, loving, living, from this centre.

☙

In the highest character-building, such as we have been considering, there are those who feel they are handicapped by what we term *heredity*. In a sense they are right; in another sense they are totally wrong. It is along the same lines as the thought which many before us had inculcated in them through the couplet in the

New England Primer: "In Adam's fall, we sinned all." Now, in the first place, it is rather hard to understand the justice of this if it is true. In the second place, it is rather hard to understand why it is true. And in the third place there is no truth in it at all. We are now dealing with the real, essential self, and, however old Adam is, God is eternal. This means you; it means me; it means every human soul. When we fully realize this fact we see that heredity is a reed that is easily broken. The life of every one is in his own hands and he can make it in character, in attainment, in power, in divine self-realization, and hence in influence, exactly what he wills to make it. All things that he most fondly dreams of are his, or may become so if he is truly in earnest; and as he rises more and more to his ideal, and grows in the strength and influence of his character, he becomes an example and an inspiration to all with whom he comes in contact; so that through him the weak and faltering are encouraged and strengthened; so that those of low ideals and of a low type of life instinctively and inevitably have their ideals raised, and the ideals of no one can be raised without its showing forth in his outer life. As he advances in his grasp upon and understanding of the power and potency of the thought-forces, he finds that many times through the process of mental suggestion he can be of tremendous aid to one who is weak and struggling, by sending to him now and then, and by continually holding him in the highest thought, in the thought of the highest strength, wisdom, and love.

The one who takes sufficient time in the quiet mentally to form his ideals, sufficient time to make and to keep continually his conscious connection with the Infinite, with the Divine life and forces, is the one who is best adapted to the strenuous life. He it is who can go out and deal with sagacity and power with whatever issues may arise in the affairs of every-day life. He it is who is building not for the years, but for the centuries; not for time, but for the eternities. And he can go out knowing not whither he goes, knowing that the Divine life within him will never fail him, but will lead him on until he beholds the Father face to face.

He is building for the centuries because only that which is the highest, the truest, the noblest, and best will abide the test of the centuries. He is building for eternity because when the transition we call death takes place, life, character, self-mastery, divine self-realization, – the only things that the soul when stripped of everything else takes with it, – he has in abundance. In life, or when the time of the transition to another form of life comes, he is never afraid, never fearful, because he knows and realizes that behind him, within him, beyond him, is the Infinite wisdom and love; and in this he is eternally centred, and from it he can never be separated. With Whittier he sings:

> *"I know not where His islands lift*
> *Their fronded palms in air;*
> *I only know I cannot drift*
> *Beyond His love and care."*

❧